Persons of the Passion

Persons of the Passion

R. Earl Allen

BROADMAN PRESS
Nashville, Tennessee

Library of Congress Catalog Card Number: 72–90040
Dewey Decimal Classification: 225.92
Printed in the United States of America

Dedicated
to
our staff who has greatly helped in the ministry of our church
and especially to those young men who have shared "study
time" with me.

J. Dan Cooper
Gordon Smith
Aubrey Howell
John Tanner
Eugene Nail
Don Worthington

Say I was there
Taking it in,
Where would you put me?
Standing and weeping with
  Mary
    Mary
      and John?
Sitting in the bleacher section
With the clowns
Hurling insults at holiness?
Kneeling by the upright,
Waiting my turn at dice?
You're wrong.
I would have been streaking down the road,
Robe aloft, elbows like pistons,
Cutting toward a Roman culvert
And diving under it.

Which makes it all the more, you see,
A work of supernatural Grace
For a faithful, saving Lord
To pull me out
And spin me round
And send me back.

—Sherwood E. Wirt

(From *Decision*, copyright 1967 by The Billy Graham Evangelistic Association)

Preface

Who could justify another book concerning the passion week of our Lord? Neither can this writer. Yet ever since our first Easter Preaching Series at the First Baptist Church, Seagraves, Texas, these messages have been in heart and mind. Now, twenty-five years later, they are committed to print. With them goes the prayer that through these personalities around the cross we may find ourselves there.

Our thanks would be first to those who heard the devotionals prayerfully and encouraged us. We dedicate these messages to those who share in the ministry of God's call to service. The eager minds and the wonderful attitudes and abilities of those who serve with us makes our work a journey of joy.

We acknowledge the continued encouragement of our friend and editor Bill Cannon. We thank with deep appreciation Miss Arline Harris and Mrs. Alfred Brian, Jr., for seeing these pages through the journey from the pulpit to the press.

R. Earl Allen

Contents

1. **PRIESTS . . . who framed Him**   13
    Unreligious Acts of the Religious

2. **JUDAS . . . who betrayed Him**   23
    The Treacherous Traitor

3. **HEROD . . . who mocked Him**   33
    Preaching That Displeased

4. **PILATE . . . who sentenced Him**   41
    The Politics of Pilate

5. **PILATE'S WIFE . . . who feared Him**   49
    The Disturbing Dream

6. **BARABBAS . . . who was swapped for Him**   57
    The People's Choice

7. **PETER . . . who denied Him**   63
    The Courageous Coward

8. **SIMON OF CYRENE . . . who carried His cross**   71
    Compelled Compassion

9. **SOLDIERS . . . who humiliated Him 77**
   Beyond the Call of Duty

10. **THIEVES . . . who called out to Him 85**
    Three Crosses and Two Thieves

11. **JOHN . . . who loved Him 91**
    Standing By the Savior

12. **THE CENTURION . . . who confessed Him 99**
    An Unexpected Declaration

13. **THE MARYS . . . who mourned Him 105**
    The Faithful Few

14. **SECRET DISCIPLES . . . who buried Him 115**
    The Prolonged Confession

15. **THOMAS . . . who still doubted Him 123**
    "I Want to Believe!"

1
PRIESTS
. . . who framed Him

Unreligious Acts of the Religious
John 18:19–24; Matthew 26:57–68

For any important news event, we have what is called "on the spot" reporting. What would such reports have been like that day in Jerusalem when Jesus of Nazareth was crucified?

First, we might have a feature story on the words uttered by that controversial figure on the center cross. They were strange, unexpected, and disturbing utterances.

A prayer: "Father, forgive them, for they know not what they do!"

An assurance: "Today shalt thou be with me in Paradise"—to a dying thief who called him "Lord."

A concern: "Behold thy mother," to a leading disciple, and, "Woman, behold thy son!"

A question: "My God, my God, why hast thou forsaken me?"

An agony: "I thirst!"

A declaration: "It is finished!"

A committal: "Father, into thy hands I commend my spirit."

We are familiar with these words. We are familiar with pictures of three crosses, the figures and faces of the men dying there, Jesus in the center. Such paintings show a crowd of people looking up at the crosses—their backs, not their faces.

13

One artist, who desired a new insight, painted his version of that scene from the other side, showing the backs of the crosses and the uplifted faces of the people. He entitled it, "Were You There?"

We have a familiar spiritual by that title, and it seldom fails to move us as we, in imagination, become one of that crowd.

> Were you there when they crucified my Lord?
> Were you there when they crucified my Lord?
> Oh! sometimes it causes me to tremble, tremble, tremble.
> Were you there when they crucified my Lord?

If we really were there, walking around in the midst of those gathered on that rocky hillside, what would we hear people saying? What would we guess of their reactions? Most of all, would we be able to identify with them? Some were merely curious and actually indifferent. Some were honestly confused. Who *was* this unusual man? Some were Roman soldiers, doing what they were commanded to do. Some were hostile.

In the forefront of the crowd were Temple priests, the rulers of the Jews—by permission of Rome—in religious matters.

Let us establish in our minds the difference between being religious and being Christian. One of the places this was most obviously demonstrated was at the crucifixion of Jesus Christ.

It has been said that one is all right as long as he is religious. But if you believe "being religious" is enough, are you not vindicating those individuals who put the Savior to death? No group ever gathered on the face of the earth was more "religious" than the Pharisees of Jesus' day. They observed every "jot and tittle" of the Law, left nothing undone, crossed every *t* and dotted every *i.*

They were religious indeed, but they had no understanding of the spirit of the law and little compassion for their fellowmen. They were cold, sinful, and proud. In the worst sense of the term today, they were "The Establishment." They were so pious they could not believe that anyone who differed with them in the least might be right. They declared that any other worship except in "their" Temple according to "their" rules was wrong. Any other claim to righteousness was heresy to them.

Even today, "Self-complacency is the nemesis of much spiritual power," said Samuel J. Schreiner. "The Pharisee who thanked God that he was not as other men, closed the door to God's mercy and grace, because he trusted in himself that he was 'righteous, and despised others' (Luke 18:9). The self-complacent people have chosen between their own legalistic interpretation of the law, which they can observe without self-commitment, and Jesus' stern system of personal behavior—love your enemies, do good to those who hate you, turn the other cheek, and refuse to retaliate for an injury. These ideals, then as now, were shrugged off because they were deemed to be unrealistic and unattainable." [1]

"Isn't it all right as long as you are sincere?" is a popular sophism today, and "I think it's all right as long as you follow your conscience." These are man's ideas—not God's. It is not enough simply that we be religious.

One can be religious in many different philosophies. Communists are religious in their zeal. There are many people who drink religiously—that is, with great regularity. You can religiously work yourself to death. You can religiously do many things. But to be Christian is something else altogether.

Christianity goes beyond the borders of denominationalism. The man who has put his trust in Jesus Christ and him alone for salvation is a Christian believer. Any other individual, regardless of background or church affiliation or religious training, who depends on anything more or anything less than faith in Jesus Christ, may be religious but is not Christian, according to the Scriptures.

Religion is not enough. And a conscience can become so blighted and scarred and hardened that it is no longer a safe guide. Conscience is not enough.

When God sent his Son down from heaven, worship was at a low ebb in Israel; the people had little respect for holy things. The priests, honored servants of the Law and of the Temple, had grown away from the people and away from God. Proud of their lineage, they felt that the Temple belonged to them and should contribute to their personal profit.

God had condemned such conduct on the part of their forefathers. "Son of man," the Lord had said to Ezekiel, "prophesy against the shepherds of Israel, prophesy, and say unto them, Thus saith the Lord God unto the shepherds; Woe be to the shepherds of Israel that do feed themselves! should not the shepherds feed the flocks?" (Ezek. 34:2). Yet Israel's spiritual leaders continued to drift far away from God.

Prejudice of the Priests

The priests were not only proud, they had great prejudice. When Jesus first began preaching, they raised the question, "Can any good come out of Nazareth?" Later, they criticized him as unlearned. They objected to his training. They had the idea that nobility and religious relationships depended on where you were born and who your parents were.

Their prejudices kept them from seeing the truths God wanted them to see. It is a sinful disease. Each of us is endowed with more of it than we recognize. Many people are prejudiced in favor of a political party. It is easy to understand why one is biased in favor of his church. But there has come a dark hour of social prejudice in our own nation, and I do not offer any easy solution to the racial problem. I do remind you that we had better stay close to God's Word if we are going to be Christian in our attitude.

In Jesus' time, those who claimed to be the people of God

dismissed many who needed them by saying, "The Jews have no dealings with the Samaritans." That is, it doesn't matter about their needs, their burdens, their aspirations—the Jews simply were not going to have any dealings with them, period! You can't wash out problems that easily. Men have interlocking concerns; the world exists or dies together.

There is a Christian attitude in regard to every problem, every burden. If we look down upon those who are less fortunate, we may become the same type of stiff-necked Pharisee. People can be completely right in their beliefs and unchristian in the manner in which they proclaim and practice them. Prejudice breeds persecution, reacts upon those who cling to it, and deprives us of some of the best things in life.

The worldly philosophy that prevails today seems to be materialism coupled with a fatalistic attitude toward life. There was a time when men sat still long enough to put their thoughts on paper. But that day is gone. E. Stanley Jones on one occasion said, "It is dangerous to think differently from the group." It *is* dangerous to think unless you think with the crowd. "Society demands conformity," he said. "If you fall below its standards, it will punish you. Rise above them and it will persecute you."

One who knew said, "He who finds the lofty peaks of snow looks down on hate and enmity below."

Profit of the Priests

The priests were not only prejudiced, they were greedy for profit.

There was no more pathetic scene, any deeper sob, any more heartbreaking experience in the life of Jesus than when he went into the Temple and saw the noisy commerce there. "My Father's house is a house of prayer, but you have made it a den of thieves!" he declared. At no time did Jesus accuse those who crucified him, but he berated indignantly those who misused the house of God.

A church building is nothing more than brick and mortar, but it has been dedicated to the worship of God Almighty. He hallows and sanctifies it, and we need a revival of respect for holy vessels.

The priests of that day, Jesus said, had made God's house of prayer into a den of thieves. It certainly revealed a new low in the spiritual life of the priesthood.

Many pilgrims traveled long distances to worship in Jerusalem. They had no refrigerated trucks, no modern transportation. They wanted to make sacrifices and offerings at the Temple of God. Rather than bringing a dove or caring for a beast on the journey to Jerusalem, many people simply waited until they got to the city and purchased sacrificial animals from the priests. Originally, the selling of these animals had existed for the convenience of the people. But there came a time when the religious leaders saw they could make money out of it. Because of the scarcity of priest-approved animals (which the priests could control), everybody had to deal with them and they had a ready-made profit.

Foreign currency was also a problem. Most coins showed images of Caesar or foreign gods and were unacceptable in the Temple. The priests set up an exchange rate which was exorbitant. Merchants and money changers had turned the Temple courtyard into a carnival, hawking for profit those things needed in the public worship of God.

Jesus, in righteous indignation, picked up a whip and drove the merchants and money changers out of the Temple. They scattered in surprised terror. How could one man exert such influence? I'll tell you why! Right prevailed. They knew that what they were doing was wrong.

Could such a situation exist today? Do we serve God for profit? Does a man preach for profit? Does a layman come to church because of good public relations? Does he come to gather business, to gain prestige, to get influence? If we put in an appearance at church for any unworthy purpose, then we are as guilty as the priests in their time. Jesus cries out still in indignation against anyone who brings impurity into the worship of God.

The house of God is a place of prayer. You do not worship God without a time of preparation. There must be a settling down and getting away from the things of the world and getting ready for the things of God. The house of God is designed and dedicated so that on the Lord's Day we might have opportunity to pray and worship with reverence. Our attendance ought to be a time of prayer.

Plot of the Priests

Especially after Jesus had spoiled their profits, the priests began to plot against him: "From that day forth they took counsel together to put him to death" (John 11:53).

In Luke 3:2, we find the names of two high priests, Annas and Caiaphas. Evil old Annas was called by David Poling "a master plotter" who "represented corrupt religion." He had been deposed from the office of high priest and his five sons likewise disqualified. Caiaphas secretly contracted to marry Annas' daughter, which served the double purpose of keeping the line of family succession and elevating himself to prosperity and prestige. Caiaphas was a selfish opportunist. To him, nothing was sacred except as it became an expedient means to serve his desired ends. In John 18:13,24, we find that Jesus was taken first to Annas, the senior dignitary.

Jesus uncovered these masters of political intrigue by his meekness, love, and holiness. At one time he went so far as to sum up the whole law of God in two simple rules: "Love the Lord thy God with all thy heart, . . . and they neighbour as thyself!" (Luke 10:27). If Jesus gained a great following, he would undermine the whole system of laws and sacrifices upon which the priests depended.

"What can we do?" they asked among themselves: "This man doeth many miracles. If we let him thus alone, all men will believe on him: and the Romans shall come and take away both our place and nation" (John 11:47–48). As one has said, "They would kill him for eating corn, while they stole the Temple's golden foundations!"

The priests heard the rumors of the raising of Lazarus. Only four days previously, Jesus had ridden into the city in the midst of triumphant shouts, "The Messiah has come!" The tumultous scene in the Temple convinced them that time was running out.

"This Disturber must die, and quickly," Caiaphas said. "Not on the feast day, lest there be an uproar among the people" (Matt. 26:5). They did not know what the crowds would do, nor how strongly Jesus' friends were organized. But the events demanded action, and they had to plot their course. How to take Jesus unawares and secretly was the problem.

"Ye know nothing at all," Caiaphas said, "Nor consider that it is expedient for us that one man should die for the people, and that the whole nation perish not" (John 11:50). There was that word, "expedient." Expedient for whom? "For us!" Caiaphas cleverly draped his selfish plans in the robe of patriotism. But his words were ironic in that they were true with a far deeper meaning than he intended. It *was* necessary for one man to die for all the people, according to the Scriptures.

Judas helped the priests solve their dilemma. He came to them secretly and asked, "What will ye give me, and I will deliver him unto you?" (Matt. 26:15).

When Jesus was brought to trial before the Sanhedrin, Caiaphas still had a problem. They were without a charge deemed worthy of death either by their own court or by the Romans, and the Roman government would have to condemn Jesus to death. If, in bringing the charge, Caiaphas dwelt on Jesus' supposed opposition to civil authority, that would enlist the sympathies of the Pharisees in Jesus' favor. If he emphasized supposed Sabbath violation or neglect of traditional observances, even his Sadducees would agree with him—but not the Romans.

Suddenly the idea must have flashed into his mind. He could force Jesus to give the reason they needed. Stepping up face to face, Caiaphas placed Jesus under the most solemn Jewish oath: "I adjure thee, by the living God, that thou tell us whether thou be the Christ, the Son of God?" (Matt. 26:63).

There comes a time when we are adjured by the very name of God—and we have to choose between being Christian or merely being religious.

"I am," Jesus answered, "and ye shall see the Son of man sitting on the right hand of power, and coming in the clouds of heaven" (Mark 14:62).

Tumult split the silence like a lightning bolt; the council became bedlam. Caiaphas ripped his outer garments in wrath, his face livid with rage. Turning to the others, he cried, "Ye have heard the blasphemy: what think ye?" (Mark 14:64).

No one could doubt the overwhelming answer—death to the blasphemer!

Caiaphas charged Jesus with two crimes: that he was guilty of blasphemy and that he incited the people to rebel against Rome. The high priest used the weapons of patriotism and religion to stir sentiment against Jesus. With political maneuvers and false witnesses, he succeeded in bringing Jesus to the cross, although the verdict was actually passed by Pilate.

Whatever was expedient, whatever promised to pay off, whatever seemed to his own advantage, that Caiaphas did.

Confronting Jesus, who embodied Christianity in its purest form, Caiaphas represented formal law. They were two extremists of religion. Caiaphas had "a form of godliness but denying the power thereof" (2 Tim. 3:5), so he inevitably decreed death for Jesus. The darkness of Caiaphas could not bear the light of Jesus' love.

NOTES

1. William S. Cannon, compiler, *Every Day Five Minutes with God* (Nashville: Broadman Press, 1969), p. 140 f.

2
JUDAS
. . . *who betrayed Him*

The Treacherous Traitor
Matthew 26:1–30

Today, a great many people believe that the cross was an accident of history, not a spiritual necessity. The Bible says that "without shedding of blood is no remission [of sin]" (Heb. 9:22).

The cross was the specific purpose of God's love, God's deliberate plan by which man should be saved. We must recognize the sacrificial death of Jesus—the scope of what he did for us, the extent to which he loved us! To imprint this on our minds, we are looking closely at the people around him on the cross, knowing they were men of frailties and temptations as we are. We can find in them warnings, lessons, and enlightenment for our encouragement in this day.

There is one man in particular that none would intend to follow. Surely, each of us would feel that we would not want to be Judas.

He was called a traitor, for the word "traitor" carries the idea of turning against—a traitor to a country is one who sells out his country. Judas betrayed his relationship to Jesus as he sold out Jesus. Perhaps we could come nearer transferring the truth and applying it to our own hearts if we call Judas "the man who might have been."

The name Judas was very common among the Jews. There were

several called Judas in the Bible. Since he betrayed Christ, it has become a name accursed. That name will always be linked with what Judas Iscariot did.

James and John are common names today. Many times they have come down from fathers or grandfathers. It is likely that originally they came from the famous apostles. But who would name a child Judas, even though it originally meant "Praise to the Lord"? A man who turns against his country is called "a Judas" as a term of contempt. The name is almost synonymous with "traitor." What tragedy and failure—the "man who might have been"!

His Personality

Although we may not feel we can fully understand Judas, his personality stands out clearly.

Among the men who walked with Jesus, Judas was given opportunity of leadership. He became treasurer of the group. He walked by the side of the Master for many months, but that does not mean that he learned to know Jesus in any deep sense of the word. With all his opportunities, Judas proved unworthy, a man who could have been better, but would not.

After a study of God's Word, it is my opinion that Judas was really not a Christian. There are some who feel that he was a Christian who was backslidden. Christ said, in his intercessory prayer, "Those that thou gavest me I have kept, and none of them is lost, but the son of perdition" (John 17:12). From the very beginning, Judas remained alienated from God. He was the only disciple who was not a Galilean, and he evidently felt himself an outsider.

Then why did Judas go along with Jesus? Was he an opportunist? The Roman government oppressed the Jews with a heavy yoke and they needed a deliverer. They anticipated a king who would ride down the skies on a snow-white charger, throw the Romans out of Jerusalem, and restore a glorious kingdom to Israel. Therefore the Jews followed after many self-styled liberators who came on the scene. When Jesus started performing miracles, the masses followed him. Many turned away when they found he was not planning to set up an earthly kingdom. Judas' primary reason for associating himself with Jesus was probably his hope of the kingdom, in which he visualized himself the administrator of the treasury.

The disciples saw Jesus deal with the individual needs of the people. They lived with him, learning something of his heart. He taught them that the reestablishment of relationship with God in a spiritual kingdom was much more important than the establishment of an earthly kingdom. More important, even, than taking revenge upon the Romans and restoring their national pride!

Judas evidently yearned for an earthly kingdom, wielding power and the center of popular acclaim. Instead, Jesus' audiences declined and hostile criticism of the Master grew. Judas saw Jerusalem turning against Jesus, whose reputation was waning—and himself holding an empty bag.

Several questions that Judas asked reveal his character. Listen to a man long enough and you will always find a window into his heart. Solomon wrote of man that "as he thinketh in his heart, so is he" (Prov. 23:7).

Judas had been with Jesus for a long time when he asked the question, "To what purpose is this waste?" (Matt. 26:8). He was a materialist who measured in terms of dollars. He questioned everything—not, "How much good will it do?" but, "How much will it cost?"

Jesus was very near the end of his life. A woman in Bethany approached him at a banquet table with a box of costly ointment, something she had saved, very valuable and dear to her. The response of her heart to Jesus prompted her to pour it upon his head. Fragrance filled the room.

Judas spoke up quickly. "Why was not this ointment sold and given to the poor?"

The others were infected with his attitude. Some might have thought admiringly, "How thoughtful! What a great benefactor!" But his suggestion was wrongly motivated. It was "not that he cared for the poor, but because he was a thief, and had the bag, and bare what was put therein" (John 12:6).

"Why trouble ye the woman?" Jesus said. "She hath wrought a good work . . . in that she . . . did it for my burial" (Matt. 26:10,12).

Have we derived from this the common saying, "Give me flowers while I live"? Jesus was implying, "Don't wait until I hang on the cross. Don't rush in too late and say how much you loved, how much you wish you had done something!"

This woman broke her alabaster box. It was a precious moment because it revealed the devotion she had in her heart for the Savior. It was a glimpse into her soul: all that she had she gave to Jesus.

Against this beautiful scene Judas raised the crass question, "How much did it cost?" The other disciples joined in the argument, trying to be logical. "If she had been in her right mind," they seemed to agree with Judas, "we might have put this money to better use!" Perhaps it was here, when Christ lauded Mary for her devotion, that the situation became too much for Judas! He never understood love—not even love of his own life.

There isn't anything logical about love, and there isn't any way you can put logic into it, though you be Judas and Scrooge rolled into one. When people are in love, they do emotional rather than logical things. They sacrifice for one another. Love is not a book-keeper, and it always does the unusual.

When an extravagant gift or a noble deed exhibits the love one feels, I don't know of anything more beautiful. When through a loving spirit we get across the reflection of God's love, I don't know that energy could be put to better use.

All Jesus' disciples seemed to enter into the question—but Judas took the lead, a rebel disciple, a criticizing member of the church.

Jesus stated the principle: "Ye have the poor always with you; but me you have not always" (Matt. 26:11). The timeliness of the gift made it more beautiful.

In the *Christian Century,* a minister told how his phone rang three times on a certain Sunday morning. Three teachers called to notify him they could not teach their classes that day. One said she had a cake in the oven. The second said she and her husband had set aside the day to paint the porch furniture. The third just didn't feel like coming. Such little things to interfere with such great opportunity for service to God! Is this love?

His Plot

We can see into the heart of Judas when a little later he devised a *plot* to betray Jesus. Going to the priests he asked, "What will you give me?" He had followed Jesus, and he evidently felt that every time he got any money in the sack, they used it for something else. It was not profiting him enough!

It's tragic to try to serve Christ for profit. It's pathetic even to tithe from a materialistic viewpoint. The motive behind the giving is of primary importance. The Scriptures say, "God loveth a cheerful giver." The amount given is not the question. It is the attitude behind the gift, as well, that makes it a suitable offering in God's sight. Judas thought the band of Jesus ought to gather offerings. People ought to put in something for the miracles Jesus had been doing for them. Rather, Jesus was constantly diminishing the treasury.

The church isn't the place to save money. The church is a place to give service to a lost and dying world. We can say we have achieved only when we have met at least some of the needs about us. We have no right to exist otherwise.

When a man begins to question, "What will you give me?" his selfish heart and motive is revealed.

The priests told Judas, "We will give you thirty pieces of silver." A slave, in Jesus' day, was being sold for more than that! A working slave, an able-bodied man, was worth even more than thirty pieces of silver on the open market. So they were saying, "This man is a teacher, a philosopher, and he is not worth much."

Judas said, "Sold!"

Arthur Gossip said: "Were it not for the charge of petty pilfering one could say with assurance that by no possibility could the man have been tempted by the small bribe promised. . . . To betray Christ for anything, for the whole world, were monstrous, but for so paltry a sum! Yet, how often we too fail Christ, betray Christ, barter Christ, for trifles of no value whatsoever!"

Thirty pieces of silver is about the equivalent of eighteen dollars in money today. Bear in mind that this was Judas' evaluation of himself. He was simply selling himself out when he sold Jesus.

What caused him to do this? Misplaced faith? Perhaps. Or loss of confidence. He was ambitious to have a high place in the court of a conquering kind. When he saw that Jesus came to minister to souls as well as bodies of men, he may have wanted to force Jesus' hand into claiming the long-vacant throne of David. If he really was the Messiah, nothing serious could happen to him!

John R. Claypool has said, "I believe the real reason behind the betrayal lay in Judas' steadfast determination to back Jesus into a corner and force him to do what he wanted him to do. There is good reason to believe that Judas had ties with the Zealot party . . . highly militant and of course anti-Roman . . . So he joined Jesus with enthusiasm and expected to be 'on the inside' when the great revolution began . . . Judas decided to betray him into the hands of his enemies and thus provoke a showdown."

Why did Judas stay with Jesus until the end? A little later, there came a very sacred moment when Jesus gathered his disciples for a last ceremonial meal. You would think that only friends of Jesus would be present, but Judas was there.

"My soul is exceedingly sorrowful," the Master said. And then, "Behold, the hand of him that betrayeth me is with me on the table" (Luke 22:21). Judas was surely one of the first to ask, "Lord, is it I?"

"Thou hast said," Jesus replied.

Why did Judas ask the question? He had already betrayed Jesus, but he was wondering if he would be found out.

Why did Jesus permit a man to remain with him whom he knew was going to sell him out? That is like asking the question, "Why did God create man in the first place?" God had complete foreknowledge at the very beginning. Why did he create us, knowing that we would fall? There is a difference, however, between predestination and foreknowledge.

A parent could tell a child, "If you ride the bicycle in the street, you might get hurt." Or say to a teen-ager, "If you aren't careful driving the car, you'll have a wreck." That doesn't mean that if the thing happens the parent willed it to happen but that by past experience he knew the danger.

His Plight

Perhaps Judas expected Jesus to call on his heavenly forces, give a demonstration of his power, and escape. When Jesus looked into his face with an expression mixed of pain and love and still said, "Friend,"—horror swept over Judas. Sin changes color after it has been committed!

Judas' plight became evident when he recognized the tragedy

he had precipitated. "I have sinned," he declared, "in that I have betrayed the innocent blood" (Matt. 27:4).

Was this confession of sin repentance toward God with faith in the Lord Jesus Christ? Not likely. Judas was only sorry for his own failure and blame. Further, he went to the chief priests and said, "Take back your thirty pieces of silver! I have sinned. I was mistaken . . . about this thing!"

"What is that to us!" they asked callously. "You made your deal. Live with it!" But he couldn't, so he died with it.

When Judas found no sympathy from the priests, he did not go back to Jesus, the only place he could have gotten help. He put his confidence in others and lost.

Men are constantly being made pawns in society. There are those who use others for a little while for their own purposes, and when they become a liability, they are cast aside.

What did Jesus call Judas at the very last? "Friend, wherefore art thou come?" (Matt. 26:50).

It is difficult to understand how Jesus could continue to love one who betrayed every confidence and kissed him in the guise of friendship. How can we comprehend the bigness of the heart of God that could be gentle with a despicable man like that?

Yet we know that there was something in the heart of God that had to be just as big when he overlooked the sins of our lives. He didn't overlook them—he forgave them and cleansed them!

Jesus didn't shake this traitor and scold. Jesus said, "Friend . . ."

How do you deal with your enemy? With vengeance? The Bible declares, "Vengeance is mine, I will repay, saith the Lord" (Rom. 12:19). The world says, "An eye for an eye and a tooth for a tooth." Jesus taught that such an attitude would never win people. Instead, "Whosoever shall smite thee on thy right cheek, turn to him the other also" (Matt. 5:39).

According to the Bible, sorrow for sin must be spiritual and permanent if a person is to find true peace. Most men regret the results of their evil actions which destroy their social standing and reputation—but this is not repentance toward God.

There was no place for Judas to go. He had turned against his friends and was despised by his comrades. He "went out by himself." See his great agony as he cried out, "I have betrayed innocent blood." It was not repentance, it was only remorse.

In the case of Judas, it seemed that even Jesus could do nothing. Can it be true that there are men with whom Christ fails? Is there clay so filled with foreign substance that the Master Potter cannot mold a useful vessel from it? Alas! If Judas had been willing to be purged of the flaws in his character, if he had been willing to be made a new creature, things might have been different! Evidently Jesus had great hopes for Judas, as the possibilities were there. Some of the greatest saints of history were also the greatest sinners before they trusted Christ.

Judas went out and hanged himself. Jesus died, also, a short while later. Judas entered into a covenant with the chief priests to sell Jesus. God entered into a covenant with his Son that he would save all those that were brought to him by Jesus.

Judas died because he couldn't face himself. Jesus died because he wanted to face God with his mission accomplished. He had prayed "for them which thou hast given me; for they are thine. And all mine are thine, and thine are mine; and I am glorified in them" (John 17:9–10).

Charles Griffin described, from a church in Bucharest, Hungary, a seventeenth-century fresco portraying Judas. "There we would see the ugly, giant black figure of Satan sitting on some hot stones in Hades, holding the doll-like person of Judas, along with the infamous bag of bribe money; and Judas is weeping in remorse."

Judas failed miserably and wept bitterly and died tragically.

3
HEROD
. . . who mocked Him

Preaching That Displeased
Matthew 14:1–12; Luke 13:30–35; 23:1–12

There were several groups whose presence or influence surrounded the cross. The governmental group consisted of Pilate, Herod, and the Roman soldiers. There was the religious group: the Sadducees, the Pharisees, the chief priests. Also, there were those who were vitally interested in Jesus: his mother, the apostles, his followers. Many simply went along for the bloodthirsty ride; a basically indifferent group made up the bulk of the audience about the cross.

Herod was not there, but his influence was felt. His type still represents a multitude of people. The heritage of his hardened heart still lives. He was displeased with the preaching of the message of God in his day.

Which people demand most perfection of the church? You will hear those demands from the ungodly. The individual who has set himself at odds against spiritual things busily demands things of the church to excuse his own sins. He expects everybody to be perfect, hoping that his screaming will give them no time to examine his life. Christians are much more forgiving. They are so busy threading the needle that they do not have time to see whether their brother has to put on bifocals to see the eye of the needle.

The message of John the Baptist displeased Herod! This we would expect—if he wanted to continue his life as he was living it. For a generation, the name Herod had struck terror into all who knew them. His famous father, Herod the Great, slaughtered the children of Bethlehem hoping to kill the one who was born "King of the Jews" according to the Wise Men. The Roman Emperor Augustus said of this Herod, "I had rather be a dog in Herod's backyard than a son in his household."

This son, called Herod Antipas, hoped by another whack of the ax he would be able to destroy God's Holy One now. When he beheaded John the Baptist, he hoped this would silence the preaching that displeased. Herod the Great had missed it over thirty years ago; his son missed it with John the Baptist.

Self-indulgent described Herod Antipas. His lineage was questionable because of gross immorality in the family. The Herods were notorious for intermarriage and incest and could not accurately trace their heritage. Yet they had set themselves up as kings of Judea and Galilee, though they were only half-Jewish, at best. The Romans used them as tools.

Herod Antipas gathered around him a group of men who agreed with him. He had to have men who would say yes to the things he wanted. He could not tolerate anybody who thought for himself. He gathered a political party, called the Herodians, who applauded everything Herod did.

The Message

Reports about John the Baptist made Herod want to hear him. His dress and doings were so strange it should be entertaining as a circus sideshow or a carnival to the court. Herod wanted to see what tricks John might have to amuse him. He found John was not a trickster, but a teacher of truth. His message was unwelcome.

Herod was displeased immediately. John did not appease his vanity.

This ruler was like the people Paul described in 2 Timothy 4:3 who "after their own lusts shall they heap to themselves teachers, having itching ears." That is, always eager to hear some new thing, but not tolerating the truth. To have a man from the wilderness come into his court and disagree with him was more than Herod bargained for.

One of the great preachers of France a century or two ago was appointed king's chaplain. Shortly the king was taken by death and his son became ruler in his place. After a service, some men of the court came to the chaplain. "Your preaching is offensive to the new king," they said. "If you do not change, you may be replaced."

"He is my king when I am in my home," the chaplain replied. "When I stand in the pulpit, Jesus Christ, my King of kings, is the only one to whom I must be obedient."

John's preaching did not agree with Herod's philosophy. He touched on very sensitive things in the life of Herod. John had no more than made his introductory remarks when he turned to the king and said of Herodias, his brother Philip's wife whom Herod Antipas had taken, "It is not lawful for thee to have her" (Matt. 14:4). John spoke in open opposition to Herod's way of life. . . . Preaching that displeased!

Many people declare that they like plain speaking. I'm not so sure we really want to face ourselves that way. I find it rather difficult in the prayer closet facing my sin, don't you? We seldom welcome the idea of someone else saying that our behavior is contradictory. We may like to hear preaching against sin—if it's sin in somebody else's life. But when it gets down to the personal level and disagrees with some of the things we wish to do, that's different!

The rugged wilderness preacher, without "culture," pointed his finger right at Herod's sin: "This thing is immoral!" Herod had him thrown into prison.

The Murder

Later, after a drunken feast, Herod was lured into a public promise that led to murder.

The people with whom we spend most of our time are likely the ones who influence us most. Herod told the dancing girl she could have anything she wanted, and she asked the life of John the Baptist. The Scriptures say Herod became sorry in his heart that he had made such a rash promise. He was moved by John's words and feared him as a man of God. Yet he had made a public oath.

He had opened his mouth when he ought to have used caution. "You made the promise. You've got to stick with it!" we often hear. Herod's followers saw to it that his feet were kept tied to the fire.

Herod, in a weak moment, in a moment when sin was at its worst, in a moment when a young woman damned her own life, gave in to a so-called queen who lowered herself to vengeance. The mother was more sinful than the daughter and more sinful than her husband—when this happens, you have wrecked lives.

"Use your body to get the promise from Herod," Herodias encouraged the girl. That dance caused the death of the best man on record. Jesus said, "Among them that are born of women there hath not risen greater than John the Baptist" (Matt. 11:11). Yet this good man was destroyed by an unholy woman.

Near one of my pastorates was a place called the Heel and Tow Club. One morning from the pulpit I made a statement that one day they would find out that there were more heels in the club than toes. The next day a group called on me. They let me know they had enjoyed other sermons much more . . . preaching that displeased!

Whether preaching is popular or not is really not the test. It is not preaching unless it is the proclamation of the gospel of the Lord Jesus Christ.

Herod was displeased with John's preaching. This was not because of the principle of relationship to Christ, but rather because of the sin in his own life. So Herod put John in jail to silence him. Later, he had the preacher beheaded. He thought he was through hearing the condemning message of God.

Soon, however, rumors about Jesus reached Herod, and his guilty conscience wondered if this were John the Baptist raised from the dead. If not, he would silence another preacher.

The leaders of the Jews knew this. Some of them went to Jesus and told him, "Get thee out, and depart hence: for Herod will kill thee."

"Go ye, and tell that fox," Jesus responded, "Behold, I cast out devils, and I do cures today and tomorrow, and the third day I shall be perfected. Nevertheless I must walk today, and tomorrow, and the day following: for it cannot be that a prophet perish out of Jerusalem" (Luke 13:31–33).

In other words, Herod had no real power over Jesus. He could not put him to death as he had John the Baptist. Jesus would die at God's appointed time and place.

Herod was not the first nor the last who have tried to silence unwelcome preaching of the Lord Jesus Christ. Many have tried this. "We will remove the individual whose preaching displeases!" has often been the rabble's cry.

What was Jesus' opinion of Herod? He called him "that old fox," and it was no compliment. A fox is crafty, but evidently that is not all that Jesus had in mind. By public reputation, Herod was superstitious and immoral. Why did Jesus refer to him as a fox? Because it is also known by those who study animals that the fox is cowardly and hesitant, a predator who had rather strike in the dark than in the light.

The Mockery

When Pilate sent Jesus to Herod, that self-styled "king of Galilee" found the Son of God only an object of mockery.

"When Herod saw Jesus," the Scriptures say, "he was exceedingly glad." Why? Because ever since that soldier walked into Herod's banquet hall with John the Baptist's head on a platter, Herod hadn't slept well! His conscience nibbled at him by day and his subconscious stirred at night. "I put that man to death," he thought. "It's the same message, so it must be the same man." Superstitious Herod, when he first "heard of the fame of Jesus, . . . said unto his servants, This is John the Baptist; he is risen from the dead; and therefore mighty works do show forth themselves in him" (Matt. 14:1–2).

It would be the highest compliment of the Christian ministry if all believed that we were preaching the same message that Jesus taught and preached.

Herod was not wanting to see Jesus to gain salvation but to relieve his conscience. He had to be sure this was not John the Baptist. "He was desirous to see him of a long season, because he had heard many things of him; and he hoped to have seen some miracle done by him" (Luke 23:8).

In other words, he also wanted to satisfy his curiosity as well as his conscience.

Jesus, when he was brought into Herod's court, uttered not a word. Herod looked at him with disappointment. He could see only a simple Galilean who offered no spirit—a man not even as fiery as John the Baptist had been. He could not see the inner power of Christ that could change lives. "And Herod, with his men of war, treated him with contempt, and mocked him."

A great many people seek the emotional; they come only when

there is an unusual attraction. They are more interested in being entertained than in being challenged by preaching that tries to get down to the heart and change them.

"Jump up and down for us!" was Herod's sarcastic desire. "Amuse me!" But Jesus wouldn't open his mouth. The dignity of silence was better than any word he might have uttered.

When the world makes its little "demands" on the Christian, silence in regard to criticism is often the best answer we can give. Yet there are times when it is a sin for the church to remain silent against the evils of the day.

Herod's mockery of Jesus continued. They "arrayed him in a gorgeous robe"—the cast-off robe of a puppet king—"and sent him again to Pilate" (Luke 23:11). All the entertainment Herod's court received from Jesus was their made-up mockery.

From being an enemy of Jesus, Herod became an enemy of all people. At last he was cast off by the Romans for his self-indulgent inefficiency and exiled to Gaul.

Eventually, payday came for Herod.

The mob on Golgotha also mocked Jesus, demanding, "If thou be the son of God, come down from the cross!" Their curiosity wanted him to do something startling, something new, something to overcome their cynical disbelief. His only answer was, "It is finished!"

4
PILATE
. . . who sentenced Him

The Politics of Pilate
Mark 15:1–15

Very early in the morning the chief priests brought Jesus to Pilate, the Roman governor. Most of the night the Sanhedrin had been in session—illegally, for it was not according to the law for them to convene during the night. Those who would do evil see the necessity of doing it in a hurry, and they were making haste.

They aroused Pilate to try Jesus.

Pilate recognized the irregularity, for on the eve of a Jewish holiday his court also was not in the habit of being in session. But he was a politician, and bowed to the wishes of the priest-led multitude.

Pilate soon realized the only reason they brought Jesus to him was to ask for a death sentence. The Romans recognized the Jewish religion and allowed the conquered race certain privileges. But they would not give them the right of death penalty. In their religious court, the Jews had power to try men for heresy and for any wrong that was done against the Temple. They could sentence another Jew, but they could not put one to death.

They were thirsting for blood, Pilate knew. For any lesser punishment, they would have seen to it themselves.

Can you imagine these two men confronting each other? Pilate was irritated because he had been aroused from sleep and forced to come to his judgment seat by the demands of the Jews. Before him stood a man who had been brutally dealt with by his accusers throughout the night.

Jesus and Pilate may have been about the same age. They could have been about the same size. Yet you cannot measure these two by the same yardstick. Jesus was erect, in full command of himself. He fully evaluated the fact that his stand as the Son of God was costing his life. Never was Jesus grander than when he stood and turned the other cheek. Never was he taller than when he opened not his mouth. Never was he more noble than when they were lying about him. The chief priests accused him of many things.

He said nothing.

Pilate was not sure of himself at all. He was bending over to catch the will of the people, not rising up to catch the will of God. Already there had come a servant with a message from his wife: "Have thou nothing to do with that just man," she had warned, "for I have suffered many things this day in a dream because of him" (Matt. 27:19). Pilate was a pathetic figure of history, a man who found himself "on the spot" from the pressure of many groups.

The Accusation

The first thing Pilate asked was the charge. "What accusation bring ye against this man?" (John 18:29). Studying the trial carefully, you recognize that Pilate played more politics than justice. He asked clever questions and on one occasion he made a profound statement.

Pilate was originally a soldier. Politics got him this job. He really had little training in justice and law and no religious background in the beliefs of the Jews. He had made a career as a soldier of fortune, and the Roman government gave him a protective judgeship in Judea. There he reaped the spoils of war.

Jesus Christ, the perfect man of history, was on trial before a man used to killing rather than saving.

The court had not been in session long until it was Pilate who was on trial rather than Jesus. The historian has to try Pilate and find that he was a people-pleaser. He did what was politically expedient rather than what ought to be done.

"What is it that you want me to do to this man?" Pilate asked the Jews. Somebody had expertly incited the mob, he realized. Their minds and hearts had been turned toward blood. Crafty leaders and a crowd with a thirst for blood! They wanted the death of Jesus, but he made them put it into words.

"If he were not a malefactor," they hedged, "we would not have delivered him up unto thee." To his suggestion that they judge him according to their law, they had to admit, "It is not lawful for us to put any man to death" (John 18:30–31).

At least their anger was genuine, Pilate felt. This man must have caused them a serious problem, and here he was, standing calmly—didn't he know the seriousness of the moment? Pilate held the key to Jesus' life . . . he thought!

He turned to Jesus and demanded, "Don't you know I have the power of life and death over you?"

But nobody could take Jesus' life. "I lay down my life," he had said, "that I might take it again. No man taketh it from me, but I lay it down of myself. I have power to lay it down, and I have power to take it again" (John 10:17–18).

Look at this pompous little Roman stand there and say to the Son of God, "Don't you know that I have power of life and death over you?" It was not true. The power of life and death was not in the hands of Pilate, it was in the hands of God.

The Roman governor quickly found he had no real authority. Jesus answered him mildly but firmly, "Thou couldest have no power at all against me, except it were given thee from above: therefore he that delivered me unto thee hath the greater sin" (John 19:11).

Pilate was trying to save himself, and in so doing, he lost himself. Men often have shortsighted vision and think only in terms of what is best today rather than what is best for eternity.

Having heard their accusation, Pilate put to them a choice: "Whom shall I release unto you?" The choice was between a notable criminal named Barabbas and Jesus.

The crowd, urged on by the priests, chose Barabbas to go free. As for Jesus, "Crucify him!" they shouted.

The Question

Then Pilate asked a pathetic question, "What shall I do?" He hadn't any real direction. He was still trying to save himself by getting someone else to decide for him. Herod gave him no help. The crowd would not accept Barabbas instead, although he was a murderer and a man whose release was not in the best interests either of Rome or of the Jews.

"What shall I do?" Pilate asked. "What shall I do with Jesus?" He should have known now that he was not going to be able to please the multitude and do justice at the same time.

Pilate stood on the balcony, looking down on the blood-thirsty hypocrites and asked, "Why, what evil hath he done?"

They cried out more emphatically, "Crucify Him!"

For the third time Pilate looked for a way to set Jesus free. He had his soldiers take Jesus and scourge him.

This meant to take a multiple-thonged whip with little pieces of lead tied into the ends and strike his back thirty-nine times (forty times less one, as the law required). Then Pilate showed Jesus again to the crowd and said, "Behold the man!" He was already half dead. Wouldn't they be satisfied? Would they settle for that?

Jesus was a pitiful figure by that time. A mock-king, with a crown of thorns and a faded purple robe, rejected and miserable to see. Pilate tried to shame them into letting him go. He was, in effect, saying: "Look at him! Can you see any further threat in such a pathetic man?"

He hoped that the very sight of the beaten, bruised, bloodstained figure would cool down the boiling emotions of the Jews and their leaders.

But it only whetted their blood-lust. "Crucify him!" they shouted repeatedly. They were determined to have his life.

"Let him be crucified!" the crowd yelled. "His blood be on us, and on our children" (Matt. 27:25). If there has ever been any prophecy come true in the mid-Eastern world, it is that: "His blood be on us and our children!" Pilate asked for their decision, and they told him.

Even to the end, Pilate still played politics. Now he had his mind made up that he was going to save himself first. If he could save Jesus at the same time, he wanted to do that. But not at any cost to him. If it was a question of saving Jesus or saving his own hide, Jesus would lose.

The Jews would not let him set Jesus free. "If thou let this man go," the priests shouted, "thou art not Caesar's friend: whosoever maketh himself a king speaketh against Caesar!" (John 19:12).

Then Pilate could no longer play politics; he could no longer hedge, he had to do something. When men are faced with a choice, and the pressure is on, they react differently. Some are calm, and it seems that the greater the pressure the more alert they are. Pilate wasn't having an easy time because he was not sure of his ground. He was a pawn of these people and he knew it. If he set Jesus free, as he knew in his heart he should, it would be at great political loss to himself, as the judgeship was a political plum.

Pilate had found the Jews troublesome from the very beginning.

Three times already they had protested to Rome concerning Pilate's actions. They were threatening him, for between the lines they were saying that he either went along with them—or else!

Pressure can also bring out the worst in men. Pilate looked at this group, knowing they hated him. Yet even the constantly bickering Pharisees and Sadducees were cooperating because they wanted something from him. Never had toleration been achieved in such a mismatched marriage of expediency!

Someone has written, in the first person, "Pilate, you were the judge who handled the trial of Jesus, the last legal link between Christ and crucifixion. We picture you as a cold, cynical agnostic, who only cared to save his own skin and reputation in Rome. You know what really bugs us, Pilate? It's that you showed Christ respect that day. You declared Jesus innocent, but in the same breath you gave him up to die. Now history tries *you!*"

The Decision

Pilate was not the only politician who has gone down trying to save himself at the expense of Jesus Christ. He let others force his decision.

"So Pilate, willing to content the people . . . delivered Jesus . . . to be crucified" (Mark 15:15).

Pilate made a coward's choice. He said, "Bring some water." Ceremonially, he held his hands over the bowl. "I am innocent of the blood of this just person," he declared. "See ye to it!" (Matt. 27:24). Symbolically, he washed his hands. Actually, there is not enough water in the seven seas, although three fourths of the world's surface is covered with water, to wash the blood-guilt off Pilate's hands, because he willfully sent Jesus to death to save himself.

"Here is Pilate, the hardheaded, hardhearted Governor of Judaea and representative of the great Caesar," Francis W. Dixon described the scene. This man "is faced with a tremendous decision, and the voice of conscience is thundering in his soul. He stands before the great crowd of people, . . . and he washes his hands in the water as if to say, 'I am free from the blood of this man whom I believe to be innocent.' What a dramatic scene this is!"

What will you do with Jesus which is called the Christ? For two thousand years that question has been re-echoing in the hearts of men.

"You may try to ignore Jesus, to refuse to make a decision about him," said Herschel H. Hobbs on the *Baptist Hour* a couple of years ago. "But that is impossible. . . . He is the unavoidable one. Sooner or later you must champion his cause or reject him. Indeed, to try to ignore him is to refuse him. You still have him on your hands."

In Hamilton, Ontario, the picture "Christ Before Pilate" was on display. A rough sailor came to the door and asked: "Is Christ here? How much to see Christ? . . . I suppose I'll have to pay it!" He sat down. Later, he took off his hat and studied the picture for an hour.

"I came here to see Christ because my mother asked me to," he said, finally. "I never believed in such things, but the man who painted that picture, he must have believed it."

History still tries Jesus, and they, as Pilate, have to say, "I find no fault in him."

5
PILATE'S WIFE
. . . who feared Him

The Disturbing Dream
Matthew 27:1–19

Have you ever dreamed about God? Probably everyone, at some time, thinks seriously or vaguely about Jesus. Claudia, the wife of Pilate, the governor of Judea, had a strange dream concerning Jesus, which disturbed her greatly.

The Romans had a superstitition that every dream of the early morning would come true. When Claudia sent word to Pilate, he recognized that this was important to her. Because of her disturbance and his curiosity and superstition, it had a strong effect upon him.

Pagan superstitions and Oriental customs had great power over even the educated minds of the day. Claudia was very troubled.

In the Old Testament, Abraham had a dream, and he started on a long journey in obedience to God, not knowing whither he went. Jacob had a dream, of a ladder into heaven, that stayed with him the rest of his days. Joseph's brothers mocked him, "Behold, the dreamer cometh!" Later, he was taken out of prison and brought before Pharaoh because he was reputed to be a discerner of dreams.

Daniel interpreted momentous dreams for the king of Babylon. In the New Testament, Joseph, the carpenter of Nazareth, learned the true parentage of Mary's child in a dream. Also, because of another dream, he took the child and Mary into Egypt, escaping Herod's massacre.

Can Providence possibly deal with us through dreams? Sometimes the only way God has of dealing with us is as we are—taking what we are and using what we have. Here God supernaturally revealed to this Gentile woman the truth about Christ.

She actually used six Greek words, "Nothing between thee and that righteous," in her message to her husband, although we have thirty-eight words in the English New Testament. One verse, Matthew 27:19, outlines a triangle of personages that made history: Pontius Pilate, the governor, Claudia Procula, his wife, and Jesus of Nazareth.

Claudia

Claudia had to be an unusual woman. Traditionally, she had a great heritage. She was the granddaughter of Caesar Augustus and became the wife of Pilate, the Roman Procurator of Judea.

It was against Roman policy for a provincial governor to have his wife with him on assignment, especially in such a troubled area. Because of Claudia's powerful family connection, she was able to go with her husband. History would say that she must have loved him greatly. Otherwise, she would never have given up social life in Rome for the unpleasant conditions that existed in Judea. Many women welcomed the opportunity to have a real reason not to be "exiled" from Roman "culture." It was not expected of her to live in the hot, overpopulated, underprivileged province even for a season. But Claudia chose to go.

She recognized the responsibility of her position and the penalty of trying to influence a judge, even her husband, in his duty. But she felt she had received a special revelation and recognized that she had responsibility toward her husband. Her dream revealed the person of Christ and Pilate's rightful position with respect to Christ.

If Claudia ever saw Jesus, we do not know. Or what experience, if any, she might have had with him previously or with his message. There is nothing in the New Testament that tells us if Jesus had influenced her. It could have been the case of the believing wife and the unbelieving husband.

I wish that we could be positive concerning Claudia's relationship to Jesus. However, we have an indication of her interest. We see her conviction that this was no ordinary man. We also hear her saying good things about the Son of God.

The Greek Orthodox Church has made a saint of this woman. They observe, even today, an unusual feast in her honor. Other groups look upon this as a conversion story, but there is nothing to corroborate that in the New Testament. One would like to think that as she sought the truth, she finally came to believe in Jesus. But we cannot be sure.

The motive of an individual is always the acid test. Really, the question is, Was she trying to save Jesus or trying to save her husband?

Jesus

Let us look again at Jesus. Whatever else we say about Claudia, we must recognize that she was the only one who had a good word for Jesus Christ after his capture until his death.

Before his arrest in Gethsemane, he had a lot of friends. Three days after his death he had friends again. But at this crucial time, he was forsaken by most of them. Even Peter, for a time, was not sure that he wanted to be identified with Jesus.

We are reminded that the centurion had something good to say about Jesus. But remember that Jesus was dead when the centurion said it!

Claudia wrote to her husband, "Have thou nothing to do with that just man: for I have suffered many things this day in a dream because of him" (Matt. 27:19). She didn't say, "Avoid him." She said, "Have nothing to do with him!" She only wanted her husband to take no responsibility for his sentencing.

Harold L. Fickett said, "Regarding Pilate's rightful position with respect to Christ, it was 'nothing between thee and that Righteous.' This is every man's rightful position. But Pilate let much come between him and Jesus, as a result of which he sent Jesus to the cross."

Even as a prisoner, there were some men to whom Jesus refused to speak. He did not answer some of the chief priest's questions. Herod taunted him, prodded him, mocked him. Jesus would not answer a single word. Evidently Pilate had some quality that appealed to Jesus.

"Art thou the King of the Jews?" Pilate asked.

"Thou sayest," our Lord replied.

Why did Jesus speak thus to Pilate? Who knows, unless it could simply be showing his compassion. We are surmising, knowing how Jesus reached out to Judas in the last moments and called him "friend."

We wonder if he saw in Pilate a desire to do right even though he was incapable of the great choice that would have caused him to be an honored man. Many men fall short of being great by being unwilling to make a decision. We cannot say that Pilate was the greatest of all governors, even though he found no fault in Jesus. He didn't have the stuff! He didn't have the moral fiber and the stamina for greatness. When the going got rough, he went with the crowd. He would not stand up alone.

Jesus may have spoken to Pilate because he recognized that even though this man was weak he wanted to do right.

"Thou sayest," Jesus replied to his question. In other words,

Pilate had hit on his true character. Jesus added, "My kingdom is not of this world," thus identifying himself as the Son of God, if Pilate had heeded the truth. But why did Jesus say these things to Pilate when he would not speak to Herod and answered the chief priest only under oath? Was this not an effort to encourage Pilate? The question is left unanswered.

Pilate

Let us examine Pilate further. His wife, feeling her responsibility deeply, let Pilate know how she felt. It was not just a woman's whim. Surely he must have recognized this. It was evidently some supernatural impression or divine intervention that found response in a sensitive woman. She had the responsibility of letting her husband know. Pilate had the responsibility for acting on the information.

The Roman governor tried strategy to escape sentencing Jesus. He sent him to Herod of Galilee, self-styled "king of the Jews." He tried to tire out Jesus' accusers running them from one court to another to determine who would take jurisdiction. This did not succeed. Neither did his offer of Barabbas as an unwelcome choice.

Pilate's past began to catch up with him. The leaders of the Jews, knowing that he had been walking a tightrope all during his administration, began to blackmail him. He had compromised many times before, pleasing one and then the other, while playing one party against the other. Now they played him against Caesar. "If thou let this man go, thou art not Caesar's friend," they declared. "Whosoever maketh himself a king speaketh against Caesar" (John 19:12).

Being a man who had been able to step back and forth across the line all his life, Pilate thought he could do it at this important time. But the man who vacillates will stumble.

Although Pilate asked Jesus, "What is truth?" he didn't really want to know. He asked it cynically.

All we remember about Pilate now is what he did, not what he said. History will always place him in the context of the Disciples Creed, that Jesus was "crucified under Pontius Pilate." That is how we remember the man.

A German novelist, Gertrud von le Fort, used the phrase as the thread of Claudia's dream in her book, *The Wife of Pilate*.

"I found myself in a dim room," the writer imagined Claudia telling her maid, "where a great number of people were assembled and appeared to be praying, . . . I heard distinctly the words: 'Suffered under Pontius Pilate, was crucified, died, and was buried.' " She could not understand how her husband's name had come to be upon the lips of those people.

Claudia seemed to hear the phrase through scene after scene, with descriptions of churches and worship practices down the centuries. "I ran, I ran as though hounded by furies; farther ever farther," she finished. "It seemed to me as though I had hurried through centuries and must hurry through centuries more, spurred on to the end of time, pursued by that dearest of names as though it concealed a destiny, immeasurably heavy, threatening to shadow not only his precious life, but that of the entire human race." [1]

Pilate tried theatrics. Dramatically, he asked the servants to bring him a pitcher of water. He stood before the multitude and washed his hands in a way actors and orators have imitated ever since. It made a vivid impression on men's minds and has been repeated in history and literature countless times. But Pilate's hands were still dirty . . . still guilty of blood.

How did Pilate die? We do not know. The man who failed so miserably is not mentioned again. Tradition has tried to make a lot of his life. One says that as an old man he became so hardened that when someone asked, "Pilate, what do you think of Jesus now?" he asked blankly, "Who is Jesus?"

Novelists have been searching for a long time, wondering what to do with Pilate. There isn't much you can do with a man who dishonors himself and rejects God. You just have to let him alone and let him die. Fiction has it that he committed suicide in the Alps and that his ghost remains restless still, being seen in the waves of the snow.

We like best to remember Pilate by his words, "I find no fault in this man." But we have to judge him by his deeds, not words. In spite of his wife's faithful words concerning "that righteous man," he delivered Jesus to the crucifiers.

NOTES

1. Gertrud von le Fort, *The Wife of Pilate,* trans. Marie C. Buehrle (Milwaukee: Bruce Publishing Company, 1957), p. 10 ff.

6
BARABBAS
. . . who was swapped for Him

The People's Choice
Matthew 27:11–16

From the beginning of time, men have been free to make choices. We are not only free to choose, sometimes circumstances force us to choose. Free to make a choice—forced to make a decision! Often it seems we have to choose between the lesser of two evils.

Never in all Christendom, never in all history has a man been forced to consider two such opposites as when Pilate put before that Jewish crowd Barabbas and Jesus. Pilate understood that he was being manipulated by the Jewish hierarchy, and this was one of his attempts to circumvent them by giving the crowd a choice.

Pilate remembered an established custom, that at the Passover he was supposed to release a prisoner as a sign of mercy. Normally the Jews presented to him the name of some prisoner they wished released. Such a prisoner would usually be one of little consequence, one whom it was no problem for Rome to release, someone not guilty of a serious crime.

The Jews had asked this privilege from the Romans as a symbol, a bow to their religious beliefs, a token of their historic celebration of escape from Egypt. Under Rome, they were a conquered province but not actually in bondage, as in Egypt. To keep that freedom alive in their hearts, and as a token of their religion, the prisoner who was released was a symbol commemorating their national release from bondage.

The Roman Government had consented and all had gone well. Now the Sadducees and Pharisees turned this good thing to their foul purposes. Pilate attempted to give the people a choice, and it was turned against him. They had no intention of letting him choose to release Jesus. However, this does not absolve Pilate. Actually, he could have, by the authority of Rome, turned down their request. Rome, at that time, wouldn't have given the snap of their fingers for the difference between the two prisoners. In fact, they might have preferred the release of Jesus.

The Convict

The convict, Barabbas, had a long history of sedition, robbery, and murder. The Romans and the Jews both knew him and understood why he was condemned as an enemy of society.

In the case of Jesus, the Jews had to move swiftly. Less than twelve hours passed from the time the Temple guards arrested Jesus in the garden until the Roman soldiers nailed him on the cross. The Jewish leaders approached Pilate in the early hours of the morning, asking him to come outside. A Jew would not go inside Pilate's palace during a feast day, for he was a Gentile, and it would make them "unclean" for the approaching Passover, according to Jewish law.

They were playing cat and mouse with Pilate, making him run their errands. They were asking him, as governor, to bend to them, and he was not enjoying it. He therefore bartered an exceptional deal—"a notable prisoner, called Barabbas" (Matt. 27:16).

Who was this Barabbas? Strangely enough, we have some reason to believe that he may have been the son of a teacher, perhaps a scribe of the law of God. His father may not have been a practicing rabbi, that is, with the watchcare of a flock, but he was a teacher

of the Jewish ceremonial law of his day. Likely young Barabbas
knew all the statutes and history of the Jewish nation.

Evidently within Barabbas burned the desire to do away with
Roman injustice to his people. In the name of so-called religious
patriotism and national freedom, he convinced himself that he
should become a leader of rebellious zealots.

Now Barabbas had been captured, tried, and was waiting in
prison. Here was a man distinguished by one thing—lawlessness.

John wrote his epitaph in five words: "Now Barabbas was a
robber." John, the apostle of love, always tried to see the best in
people, but he was at a loss for good words about Barabbas. Luke
was very frank to say that he "for a certain sedition made in the
city, and for murder, was cast into prison" (Luke 23:19).

A thief and a robber are not quite the same. A thief steals in
a cunning manner, without violence. A robber is one who would
do violence to take something by force that belongs to another. In
certain circumstances, a robber often becomes a murderer. Therefore we see how Barabbas made his reputation. Mark says Barabbas "lay bound with them that had made insurrection with him,
who had committed murder in the insurrection" (Mark 15:7).
Many have tried to identify him as a Jewish patriot—one of the
"good boys" of a cause. He is more truthfully just the man in cell
number 1, distinguished by his sins.

Barabbas practiced the art of killing any Roman when he had
the opportunity. He thought that he had the right to do so as a
"patriotic" Jew. Many self-styled messiahs had risen up against
Rome, claiming to be the savior who was to liberate the Jews.
Barabbas had evidently hoped to gain allegiance and power to free
his people from the Romans. Some of Jesus' disciples had perhaps
dreamed of the same thing. "We hoped that it had been he [Jesus]
who should have redeemed Israel," said the despondent men on
the Emmaus Road.

The Contrast

Barabbas was the picture of a thief, wanting a material, political, and physical route to power! Jesus took a very different way. He was not saying a word, not violent or rebellious, making no accusations. Jesus had said of false shepherds, "He that entereth not by the door into the sheepfold, but climbeth up some other way, the same is a thief and a robber" (John 10:1). The Jews chose a robber instead of the one who was "the way" for them. He was also "the door" for true release from slavery to freedom. The contrast was great.

Pilate, comparing the two opposites, asked, "Whom will ye that I release unto you? Barabbas, or Jesus, who is called Christ?" (Matt. 27:17).

They said, "Barabbas!"

The most natural reaction any man ever made was Pilate's shocked question, "Why? What evil hath he done?" (Mark 15:14). The governor-judge was surprised by the action of the jury-mob, for they had been swayed by influence rather than evidence. They had acted on faults rather than by facts because of the insistent urging of the priests.

The crowd demanded Barabbas, an avowed enemy of society.

Jesus was a sufferer for society. Barabbas suffered *by* society, while Jesus suffered *for* society. One broke the law, the other fulfilled the law. One was an enemy of man and God, the other a friend of God and man. One robbed God, while the other robbed himself when he took upon himself the form of man. One took life and one gave his life that others might live. Between those two, which would the people choose . . . Barabbas or Jesus?

A great scholar of the New Testament says that a strange thing here was that likely Barabbas also bore the name "Jesus." It was not uncommon, as among some races today, to use the name

"Jesus." Could Pilate have addressed the mob that day by asking, "Which will you take—Jesus Barabbas or Jesus the Christ?"

The Choice

This was the choice that faced the people. Barabbas-choices are still made in life. Anything that comes between us and Christ could be referred to as "a Barabbas." Most Christians, even, love something better than they love Christ: pride of appearance, fame, worldly pleasures, riches, sinful recreations, lust, possessions—the list is almost endless! When we are faced with a choice between Christ and Barabbas, with Pilate, we often wash our hands and turn away.

These two thousand years later the facts have not changed. Nobody has brought in any evidence whatsoever that would change the circumstances from when Pilate stood there and said, "Whom will you have, Jesus Barabbas or Jesus the Christ?"

Pilate asked the question with desperation.

The full context of the crowd's answer must be taken into consideration: "Let his blood be on us and on our children!" What about the blood of Jesus? It is true that "without shedding of blood is no remission" (Heb. 9:22). In Christ there is life. In Barabbas there is death. Between Christ and Barabbas, the choice of life or death is made.

Barabbas could boast, "I am the man whose place Jesus took. He was my substitute."

As Edwin McNeill Poteat, a modern American clergyman and author has put it in a poem, "Barabbas Speaks,"

> I heard a man explaining
> (they said his name was Paul)
> how Jesus, on that fateful day,
> had died to save us all.

> I found it hard to follow
> His finespun theory,
> but I am very, very sure
> He died that day for me.[1]

What, really, were the reactions of Barabbas when he heard the good news? I imagine he thought Jesus was a fool, and thought no more of it than that. We do not know if he ever accepted Jesus Christ as his substitute for sin.

The late John McNeill said that of all the people in Jerusalem, he thought Barabbas had the best idea of the atonement of Jesus Christ. "Until you can give a better theory of the atonement," Dr. McNeill said, "take that of Barabbas—Christ your substitute, dying in your place."

NOTES

1. James Dalton Morrison, ed., *Masterpieces of Religious Verse* (New York and London: Harper and Brothers, 1948), No. 578.

7
PETER
. . . who denied Him

The Courageous Coward
Mark 14:66–72

The faces about the cross would certainly include Simon Peter. He would probably be standing afar off, burdened with heavy remorse.

Peter's faults are not glossed over in the Bible, not even by John Mark in his Gospel, which reflected much of what that young man heard of Peter's reminisences. Simon must have remembered that night before the crucifixion and retold the story many times as a warning to himself and as a plea to others not to follow his example of self-pride. It also demonstrated Jesus Christ's wonderful love and forgiving grace.

Peter was prominent among the disciples. He was a leader and quick-spoken. The others probably admired him a great deal. He may have been most successful in the fishing business. Whatever his background, he was usually spokesman for the group.

John has been called "the beloved apostle." Most of us identify with Peter as he certainly was the most human. Strangely enough, we hear of his faults from himself rather than from his critics. His own impulsive acts and foolish words saddened him and caused him grief.

Boastful Courage

The most notable of Peter's unwise statements was his claim of unfailing loyalty to Jesus. One of his faults was boastful courage.

After about three years of ministry, Jesus began to tell his disciples that he must go to Jerusalem. he would die there and certain things would happen to them. He spoke again of his death at the Last Supper and on the way to Gethsemane. In the surprised silence of that moment, Jesus explained that some of them might deny him. "All ye shall be offended because of me this night: for it is written, I will smite the shepherd, and the sheep shall be scattered" (Mark 14:27).

Peter spoke up impulsively. "Although all shall be offended, yet will not I!" (Mark 14:29).

He forgot for that moment that he was one of a band, a close group. They had journeyed together, prayed together, and worked together. His words implied that there might be questions concerning the others, but not about himself. The Lord might not be able to depend on them, but he could depend upon Peter at all cost, on all occasions!

These words showed lack of humility on Peter's part and lack of consideration for the others. Peter cast aspersions upon the affection, faith, and loyalty of the disciples. There are many places in God's Word that say a man should guard against boasting, such as, "Let him that thinketh he standeth take heed lest he fall!" (1 Cor. 10:12). Peter suffered from the "hoof and mouth disease"—he was constantly sticking his foot in his mouth, managing to say the wrong thing at the wrong time. He boasted to Jesus, as other men were listening, "You can always count on me!"

Ralph Waldo Emerson said: "A man cannot speak, but he judges himself. With his will or against his will, he draws his portrait to the eye of his companion with every word."

Simon Peter did not recognize that temptation could be so cleverly devised. He did not know how potent the devil's brainwashing could be. He did not know what suit of clothes glamorous temptation might wear. Neither had Peter recognized the pressure of society: the insidious, silent voice that says, "Everybody else is doing it! It is quite all right for you!" Peter talked big, but he had not come to the place where he was willing to stand up as an individual against the crowd. The Bible clearly said, "Thou shalt not follow a multitude to do evil" (Ex. 23:2). From Peter's words it is easy to see that he recommended himself very highly.

When Peter made his declaration aloud, he was saying by conduct, deed, and thought: "I am stronger than others. I will not fail!" Had he not already fallen, when he had come to the place where he was so sure of himself? He was not depending on the Lord's grace to stay close to him. Rather, he was sure of his physical strength, confident that he would remain faithful!

"In the crises of life," Harry Emerson Fosdick has well said, "when we have no time for long premeditation, our words show where our souls have been feeding."

It wasn't long before Peter's boast was tested. His self-assurance was tried and found wanting.

The Temple guards came to Gethsemane to arrest Jesus and the Master put up no fight. Judas reached over and kissed him with the hissing kiss of betrayal. Peter, not knowing the inner power of following his Master and not knowing anything else to do, reverted back to the action of the flesh. He had spoken words of the flesh, and he took the sword in a fleshly manner to cut off the soldier's ear.

As Hudson Taylor said: "Too often we attempt to work for God to the limit of our incompetency, rather than to the limit of God's omnipotency."

Christians do not conquer the world by the sword. Neither do they conquer by pressure. We do not win any battles by using the sword against lost men. "Put up again thy sword into his place," Jesus said, "for all they that take the sword shall perish with the sword" (Matt. 26:52).

We must recognize that we are going to die in the same manner and by the same things that we live by. You put your faith, dependence, and security on certain things, and the day will come when they are useless.

You can't help noticing Peter's inconsistency—and all of us have the same problem. Being up and down, never quite knowing at any given moment how we will react, has often been our experience. It is said that we are more like Peter than any of the other disciples. This could be true. He denied Jesus, but his denial is not as difficult to take as his boasting.

What is a temptation to one man may not be a temptation to another. To some, temptation may be a thing of constant pressure and frustration. To others that particular thing might not have any persuasiveness at all. There ought to be a reverent consideration of the reality that Satan will shake any character in any way that he can get hold.

Jesus brought Peter up close when he said, "Peter, Satan hath desired thee." Why did he desire him? Peter was always speaking for the group. Satan watched him and reasoned that if he could get hold of Peter, many would follow. If he could shake Peter up, pull the rug from under him, make him fall on his face—people would laugh at him and the testimony of the disciples would be thwarted.

In Job's day, Satan boasted to God that he walked up and down the earth among God's people. He often comes to church, you know! He wanted to shake Job, to take everything away from him and see if he could make him curse God.

The Lord defended Job, saying that Job served him out of the love of his heart and faith—not because of the material things. God allowed Satan to take away all that Job had, because God was not in his things, but in his heart!

The devil tried to shake Job, but he failed!

Jesus knew the persuasive power of Satan. "Satan hath desired to have you, that he may sift you as wheat" (Luke 22:31), Jesus told Peter. Satan will always tempt those whose fall would cause the greatest shame, the greatest burden, the greatest scandal.

"But I have prayed for thee," Jesus assured Peter, "that thy faith fail not" (Luke 22:32).

Cowardly Denial

"Lord, I will never offend thee!" Peter emphatically declared.

Then what happened? Temptation came, and he yielded. It came, once, twice, and the third time . . . then he heard the cock crow!

He had failed tragically. He had talked bravely, but he was only a courageous coward.

The third time Peter denied Jesus, "while he yet spoke, the Lord turned, and looked upon Peter." He didn't speak a word, but how much must have flashed from his eyes into the eyes of Peter. "And Peter remembered the word of the Lord, how he had said unto him, Before the cock crow, thou shalt deny me thrice" (Luke 22:61).

What did Jesus' look say? Was it a look of scorn? Or of hatred? Did it say, "You've had your chance and lost it!" Was it a look of rebuke? Surely there was love and tenderness and kindness in Jesus' look that went all the way through the heart of Peter. "And Peter went out, and wept bitterly."

> The cock crows coldly.—Go, and manifest
> A late contrition, but no bootless fear!
> For when thy final need is dreariest,

> Thou shalt not be denied, as I am here;
> My voice to God and angels shall attest,
> Because I KNOW this man, let him be clear.
>   —ELIZABETH BARRETT BROWNING

Jesus had taught Peter about forgiveness some days before. "Lord, how oft shall my brother sin against me, and I forgive him?" Peter had asked. "Till seven times?" That was what the Jewish Law required.

Jesus answered, "I say not unto thee, until seven times; but, Until seventy times seven" (Matt. 18:21–22). Just keep on forgiving!

Someone could have taken Peter out and tied him to a stake and beaten him until he fell unconscious, and likely it wouldn't have hurt him as much as that loving look of Jesus.

What had happened to Peter? Looking back, we remember that he was with Jesus in the garden of Gethsemane. How much comfort it was to Jesus, we are not sure. At least Peter and the others were with him physically. But then Peter went to sleep. Spiritually he was a long way off. "Simon, sleepest thou?" Jesus said sorrowfully. "Couldest not thou watch one hour? Watch ye and pray, lest ye enter into temptation. The spirit truly is ready, but the flesh is weak" (Mark 14:37–38).

Later, after Jesus' arrest, "Peter followed him afar off unto the high priest's palace" (Matt. 26:58). He warmed himself at the enemy's fire. He kept a respectable distance as Jesus was taken out of the court to the cross.

He was too cowardly to walk in step, but too courageous not to stay in sight.

Afterwards, Peter recognized the full consequence of his sin. "He thought thereon and wept." After we sin, we discover the terrible burden it becomes—that terrible loss of fellowship, that terrible consciousness that we have wronged God. Like Peter, we slip away.

Curative Commission

On the morning of the resurrection, the angels told the women who came to the tomb, "Go your way, tell his disciples and Peter" (Mark 16:7). Peter surely needed it more than anybody else just then. He had failed himself and his Master. He was all washed up and God couldn't ever use him anymore. He felt that, because he had sinned, God had dismissed him. He didn't have another chance!

Jesus took this way of letting Peter know he wasn't overlooked by the Lord, that his denial was not held against him still.

What did Jesus tell him? A week or so later, by the Sea of Galilee, Jesus asked, "Simon, son of Jonas, lovest thou me?" He probed Peter's love, not his acts.

"Yea, Lord, thou knowest that I love thee, "Peter answered. Jesus said, "Feed my sheep!" (John 21:16).

What he was saying was that love is not measured by the manner in which you speak words; love is not measured by how much you claim. The depth of your love is made known by the manner of your faithfulness. Jesus' cure for backsliding is always service!

Jesus gave Peter a curative commission. First the unspeakable depth of love, then the job to do.

If we love Jesus, we must do something about it! Do something about the people who need him so badly. Go out and feed his little lambs, go out and feed his sheep, go out and tell men how much he loves them.

Often our words about our love for Jesus, as Peter's, are vain repetition. We must serve him in such a way that no one can deny that we love Jesus. "Your speech betrays that you have been with Jesus," they said to Peter. In this case it was his Galilean accent.

But in the case of modern man, it is the themes we accent that let people know that we have been with Jesus. They know by the words we speak, the look on our face, the faithfulness of our service.

8

SIMON OF CYRENE

. . . who carried His cross

Compelled Compassion
Matthew 27:27–37; 16:24

In today's newspaper, you will find in the want-ads section, "Positions Wanted." If you were interested in a job, you would look for attractive hours, bonuses, hospitalization, retirement benefits, and the other material attractions that seem to be so necessary in our way of life.

If you found among them a bold-face ad that said, "Wanted: Christians to Bear Crosses"—what reaction would you have? There is something in us that rebels when such a demand is made. It is very human to oppose things that are forced upon us.

Into the life of Simon, from the city of Cyrene, came something that he was forced to do. He had no choice concerning his role.

If you had your choice of all the men in history, whom would you choose to be? David, the man that God said was after his own heart? Abraham, the man who was called the friend of God? Enoch, who walked so much with God that one day God took him? Peter, who had the privilege of preaching on the day of Pentecost? Or Paul, who had such philosophy, power, and persuasion that his hearers were dumbfounded?

What if you were sitting down with Jesus and his disciples at the Last Supper? Look around the table; if he gave you the choice to blend into their lives, which one would you become? Immediately we would mark out Judas. Look at Matthew, James, John, and the others. Which one would you like to be? I suspect we might like to be the one that was talked about the most. We would probably want to be Peter. Or perhaps that disciple who laid his head upon the shoulder of Jesus.

We cannot be any of these. But in a sense we can still ask for the place of Simon, who bore Jesus' cross.

> Must Jesus bear the cross alone,
>   And all the world go free?
> No, there's a cross for every one,
>   And there's a cross for me.
>
> —SHEPHERD

Had you rather be one who bore the cross of Jesus, when needed most? When Jesus was tired and weary of body . . . beaten half to death? Had you rather be the one who literally bent under his cross and for a while took the burden? The grandest opportunity God can give any of us is to be a cross-bearer for Jesus.

The Cross Compelled

The tremendous burden that came on the life of Simon was one of the most dramatic things that happened in New Testament days. He actually, physically bore the cross of Jesus! It was a cross he was compelled to bear.

According to Julian the historian, it was the year A.D. 32, that Simon a wealthy African Jew, made a pilgrimage to Jerusalem. How long he saved up for the trip we cannot know. Evidently he desired to be in Jerusalem during the Passover season for the wonderful celebration of God's grace to his people. No doubt the man had made many sacrifices in order that he might take this special trip. He is described as a man "who passed by, coming out of the country" (Mark 15:21).

Just as he arrived at the gate of Jerusalem, he saw a mob pouring out on the road toward Golgotha. He had heard of crucifixions. He could see and hear the mob, as well as the Roman soldiers. For a moment he looked at the man falling under the weight of his cross. In front of him was carried a placard which read, "This is Jesus of Nazareth, the King of the Jews."

Suddenly, the soldiers reached out and laid hold upon this pilgrim and thrust him under Jesus' cross.

Several things had affected Jesus. He had gone without sleep all night. Already he had walked many miles. He traveled from the upper room to Gethsemane and back to the high priest's—he was taken on to Pilate, to Herod, and back to Pilate.

In Gethsemane, he had sweated great drops of blood and his heart had broken. He was already a dying man. He had suffered Judas' betrayal, Peter's denial, and desertion by the others he called friends. How disappointed could he be? Jesus was accused by the rulers of the Jews as a blasphemer. Soldiers spit in his face and mocked him. Finally, he was severely flogged until he lost so much blood he was half dead. But Jesus asked no concessions.

Why did he fall when the others did not? First of all, they were not dying of a broken heart. They were being put to death for their well-known misdeeds, while Jesus was giving his life an offering for sin. Why were they able to carry their crosses when he faltered under his? Because already he had been beaten near death, and they had not. He had undergone great emotional shock, yet he had not asked for one to take his place.

The Roman soldiers, in a hurry to get this murderous business over with, grabbed the first stranger they saw and said, "You carry his cross!"

They had been more in the providence of God than they realized. They made a man who was probably black-skinned carry the cross of Jesus. He is the Savior of all races, regardless of where they live or what color they are. Simon probably wasn't happy about this thing. The Scriptures say they "laid hold upon one Simon, of Cyrene"—that is, the soldiers forced it on him.

He had come to Jerusalem for the religious observances, and now he was having part in the cruelest of Roman so-called justice. If he wanted to go to the Temple, he would be ceremonially un-clean. He would not be able to make Passover sacrifices. His whole trip would be wrecked; he had come for nothing. But in his hurry to get down to the Temple, Simon might have missed the great opportunity to do the most religious thing that happened in Jerusa-lem, carrying the cross of Jesus.

The Cross Chosen

"Simon, you bear the cross," they demanded.

"But it's not in my plans—"

Our cross must be chosen. We may have made our plans for this week. Then God steps into our lives and says, "I want your talent, I want your ability, I want your life." Sometimes we answer, "Lord, that's not in my plans!" Our goals may be worked out, our purposes fixed, perhaps. In effect, we may say, "Lord, I'll have no time for you. My life is committed to other things." As we hurry on our busy way, we may miss the fact that God is wanting to bless us with a special privilege of service.

In going through rituals we may miss opportunities God wants us to have. Are we in such a hurry to get to Jericho that we pass by people who need to know about the Savior?

Simon of Cyrene was an innocent bystander. Being drafted to carry Jesus' cross may have caused him to reconsider his faith and his life-purpose. His sons, Alexander and Rufus, became leaders in the early church (Mark 15:21; Rom. 16:13). What had been forced upon him was freely accepted in love.

Nobody is going to grab us physically today and make us carry a cross. Bearing the cross of Jesus demands a choice. Do you take the responsibilities God offers you? When you do not take up your cross, you miss opportunities of service and reward.

We need to understand the difference between burdens and crosses. Burdens are the unavoidable circumstances of life. You may have one burden, your neighbor another, as there is no man without trouble. Job said, "Man that is born of a woman is of few days, and full of trouble" (14:1). Does this mean that such burdens excuse us from carrying the cross of Jesus? No, burdens are unavoidable, but crosses must be voluntary choices.

The Cross Commanded

"Take up thy cross," Jesus commanded us, "and follow me!" Crosses are God-given, but each of us has to accept his own cross deliberately and follow Jesus. If we magnify the cross, each finds his own place with Jesus.

To take up our cross means, among other things, to become disciples in the fullest sense of the word. It comes from the Latin expression *discipulus,* from which we derive the word "discipline." It means to be carefully trained and taught. Many thousands came to Jesus for salvation, but he chose only seventy who fully followed him and had been trained by him to preach the gospel.

Thomas à Kempis said, "Jesus now has many lovers of his heavenly Kingdom but few bearers of his cross."

For the Christian, the cross is not only a choice, it is a command! Jesus said to his disciples, "If any man will come after me, let him deny himself, and take up his cross, and follow me" (Matt. 16:24).

It has been well said that dragged crosses are always heavy, but those carried joyously are light. Jesus promised, "My yoke is easy, and my burden is light" (Matt. 11:30).

9
SOLDIERS
. . . who humiliated Him

Beyond the Call of Duty
Matthew 27:27–32; John 19:23–24

Since its birth, our country has never been occupied by foreign troops. Our people have not seen the atrocities of war—other than those in the military service. They have seen tragedies and cruelties in other parts of the world.

In ancient history, the Turks probably rank as the experts in cruelty above any other army of occupation. But Rome quickly mastered the art. They conquered many other nations with military might. However, they had a hard time conquering ideas. Hugo said that there is nothing more powerful than all the armies that have ever marched except an idea that has come to full bloom.

The Bible deals with the ideas and people of Israel. Jesus, a descendant of David, was of the Jewish race. He was among those who had been hated and despised, but the Jews fought on when neighboring nations were conquered. At last they gave up in the face of military might, but they were never willing to surrender the Hebrew concept of God. Even though they were an occupied people in New Testament times, and seemed to be a dying race, the great principle that held them together was their religion.

Soldiers of occupation have never been popular people. Our own men have seen, "Go home, Yanks!" in places where they were risking their lives for the people. However, the Roman legionaires could hardly be compared with other soldiers.

And of all places, the Roman soldiers did not want to be sent to Judea. They considered it the jumping-off place of the world, the Siberia of their time. It was isolation duty, and often the sorriest and cruelest men were sent there. The Roman soldiers stationed in Judea hated the country and particularly delighted in taking it out on the Jews.

In the Bible, we find four classes of soldiers. As far back as ancient Egypt, soldiers were organized as the body-guards of the ruler. History suggests they ate with the Pharaohs, never leaving the king's side. They were considered the elite of the nation.

Outside the capital cities were the provincal soldiers. Over each such band would be a leader the Romans came later to call a centurion. Usually he was a professional soldier and served under the governor. As conquering armies marched across the earth, their governments moved into "uncivilized" areas. The more opposition the citizens showed, the greater cruelty and the more stringent examples of punishment the conquerors used to keep down rebellion.

At a slightly later age in history, soldiers became mere adventurous mercenaries. Such men were for hire under any flag and for any cause. Known first in Egypt, many of them were slaves, fighting under the Pharaoh's promise that they would be liberated if victorious.

There came the day when ordinary citizens rallied to the needs of their country and served as soldiers on a volunteer basis. This was known as a citizen army, which could remain temporary or become a regular army.

The Israelites considered themselves a separate people, a special people, a people selected by God. The Romans worshiped Caesar and considered such a "peculiar" people proud, intolerant, and narrow. They delighted in having authority over them. The Roman soldiers never minded exercising a little extra pressure beyond the call of duty to put down the Jews.

After Jesus' birth, Herod sent soldiers to kill small children in Bethlehem. The little family of Joseph escaped to Egypt.

The Temple Guard

As Jesus approached the cross, he came into contact with four groups of soldiers. The first were the temple guards.

In the garden of Gethsemane, his disciples went to sleep. It is believed, with deepest reverence for the Scripture, that the nearest Jesus ever came to death other than when he was beaten and when he was crucified, was when he was in agony that night. He hesitated momentarily at the cup and prayed, "Father, if there be any other way—let this cup pass from me."

After a time, he waked his disciples. "What, could you not wait with me one hour?" he rebuked them sadly. Soon there came the sound of a crowd, led by Judas and the Temple guards.

Under Roman government, several authorities had their special provinces and took care of minor infractions of the law. To Rome, this was a religious question. The High Priest, who was head of the Temple hierarchy, asked that Jesus be brought to him for questioning. Annas' own personal guards, guided by Judas, found Jesus in the garden. That treacherous disciple identified Jesus by giving him a kiss of false friendship.

The Jews were prepared for opposition, but there was only one gesture of resistance. Simon pulled his sword and cut off the ear of a guard. Jesus rebuked him: "Put up again thy sword into place; for all they that take the sword shall perish with the sword" (Matt. 26:52).

Jesus picked up the ear and put it on Malchus, the high priest's servant (John 18:10). It was healed instantly.

"I am he whom ye seek," Jesus said calmly.

The guards bound him and they started back to the Temple area. We wonder what Malchus was thinking when he affixed the chains on Jesus, a man from whom he had expected opposition and who was reputed to be a revolutionary. How surprising! He had asked his own men to put up their swords and stopped to heal an enemy.

This probably made an impression on Malchus and the others that nothing else would. But I think the Lord would have done it anyway. What Malchus said—if anything—is not recorded.

The Temple guards took Jesus to Annas, then from Annas to Caiaphas. Before the Sanhedrin, Jesus faced questions and accusations. Intensity of feeling against him grew. He was taken to Pilate's judgment hall, escorted by Temple guards.

The priests asked Pilate to come outside. They were ceremonially clean for the upcoming feast. If they went inside a Gentile building, they could not celebrate the Lord's Passover.

The Governor's Soldiers

Pilate came to the balcony and held the trial there. The governor's soldiers probably took charge of Jesus. Back and forth Jesus was shuffled—over to Herod and back to Pilate. Pilate felt that Jesus was a moral man, not a criminal guilty of death. But he recognized the Jews' determination to get rid of Jesus. They would also be happy to remove him from the governor's chair. They threatened to report him to Rome, and Pilate did not want another mark against him in Caesar's book.

The governor thought of something that might satisfy the mob. He ordered Jesus flogged. "Then the soldiers of the governor took Jesus into the common hall and gathered unto him all of the band of soldiers and they stripped him and put on him a scarlet robe." That was beyond the call of duty!

Until Jesus was accused before Pilate, it was not the Romans' responsibility. It was the Jews' problem. Usually they never agreed on anything—but they joined in this strange sport of blood. Now there was a law against flogging with the whip more than thirty-nine stripes, or blows. They had tested just how much a man could stand without dying before they settled on this number. There was nothing against a Roman soldier adding extra muscle to what he was doing. With Jesus' hands tied, his back exposed, they took leather thongs into which were tied pieces of sharp metal. They could cut a man's back open like knives and leave it hanging in ribbons of flesh. There were some soldiers who took great pride in their handiwork on such a job.

"And when they had platted a crown of thorns, they put it upon his head, and a reed in his right hand: and they bowed the knee before him, and mocked him, saying, Hail, King of the Jews! And they spit upon him, and took the reed, and smote him on the head. And after that they had mocked him, they took the robe off from him and put his own raiment on him, and led him away to crucify him" (Matt. 27:29–31).

After this flogging, we can understand why Jesus fell under the load of his cross—the loss of blood, loss of sleep, humiliation, and suffering. The two malefactors, having only been in prison, were not so physically exhausted. It became necessary that someone carry Jesus' cross for him.

Evidently Pilate thought the flogging might appease the Jews so that they would not further insist on Jesus' death. They could not, under the law of Rome, take capital punishment into their own hands. Pilate was mistaken; they could not be appeased.

Golgotha's Guards

On Pilate's orders, a detachment of Roman soldiers took Jesus and the two thieves outside the city to crucify them—Golgotha's guards.

Crucifixion was used only for the occupied races, never as capital punishment for a Roman citizen. The Romans made the most of this cruel form of capital punishment. Every cross on the skyline of the Mediterranean world was an example to revolutionaries to never lift their hand against Rome! Crucifixions were staged in public places and crowds were encouraged to watch.

That was why some of the curious were there. But some were as bloodthirsty and sadistic people as ever gathered from the four corners of the earth. The place of crucifixion was outside the city, overlooking the garbage dump.

The suffering of Jesus had already been almost unbearable. This was one reason he died earlier than the others and his bones did not have to be broken to hasten death. This was according to the prophecy, "He keepeth all his bones: not one of them is broken" (Ps. 34:20).

The Master dreaded the cup. Surely he found it less humiliating to have his back torn open than to have his robe torn from him in the presence of the curious and those who loved him.

The soldiers looted whatever garments a victim might have. So they cast lots, gambling for leftover clothes. They could hear the cries of the people who were grieving over loved ones and the moans of those dying. They were caught in the middle, so they ignored both and gathered around the games they devised.

The seamless robe stripped from Jesus was probably the best prize. So they rolled the dice for it.

When Jesus said, "I thirst," he was offered a sponge of vinegar, lifted up on a reed. It had some sedative effect, and Jesus did not take it.

Did they offer it out of pity, or to quiet him? By this time he may have gained some sympathy among the soldiers, because he was probably the only man they ever crucified who did not curse them with every drop of blood that fell.

Primarily, Jesus felt forsaken because God could not look upon the sin he was bearing. It was utter humiliation to be exposed before mankind whom he had made in his own image. But even then, Jesus did not ask why he made man.

The Tomb Watch

Annas and the other priests were not satisfied. They complained to Pilate about the sign over the cross which read, "The King of the Jews." Defiantly, Pilate refused to change it.

Then they reminded Pilate that Jesus was reported to have said that after three days he would rise again. They wanted a guard, a tomb watch kept. So we find a fourth time that Jesus was under guard by soldiers. Only a broken body, but still considered dangerous!

Pilate gave them their death watch.

Evening was at hand. Jesus' body was hastily put in the tomb of Joseph of Arimathaea. Soldiers went with Joseph and Nicodemus. Jesus had a military escort even in death.

The tomb was sealed with the mark of Caesar. The seal was not to be broken. It was more than just putting a rock in place!

Another day and night passed. Then angels came, the messenger-soldiers of God. They moved away the stone. In Matthew 28, we read that the Roman soldiers were stunned and dazzled. They reported it to the priests, who told them to say that while they slept, Jesus' disciples came and stole the body away.

"And we will protect you," the priests promised.

Bribery and power spread a false story, as Roman soldiers were not in the habit of letting prisoners get away, much less losing dead bodies. When Paul and Silas were released by an earthquake in Philippi, the Roman jailer was about to kill himself, thinking his prisoners were gone.

"Do thyself no harm, we are all here," Paul said.

To a Roman guard, to lose a prisoner was to lose his own life. Their lips were sealed with the promise of wealth and of protection. Even in death, they tried to make Jesus out a liar. The Scriptures say this is the story known among the Jews until this day. The soldiers could no longer lay hands on him.

D. L. Moody often told the story of a certain elderly minister who described Peter preaching at Pentecost. He imagined a man shoving his way through the crowd.

"Peter, is there any hope for me? I made the crown of thorns and pushed it down on Jesus' head. Can I be saved?"

"Yes," said the apostle, *"Whosoever* believeth on him shall not be ashamed."

Another came and said, "I'm the man who put the reed in Jesus' hand and mocked him. Do you think he will save me?"

"Yes," said Peter. "He told us to go into all the world and preach the gospel to *every creature.* He did not mean for any to be left out."

Still another spoke up. "I am the Roman soldier who took the spear and drove it into his heart. Do you think there is hope for me?"

"Yes," was the reply. "Didn't he pray, just before that, 'Father, forgive them, for they know not what they do'? There's a nearer way of reaching his heart now: *whosoever* shall call upon the name of the Lord shall be saved!"

10
THIEVES

. . . who called out to Him

Three Crosses and Two Thieves
Luke 23:27–47

To a stranger, approaching Golgotha that fateful day, it would have seemed from all outward appearance that there were really three criminals of one sort or another.

Crosses were not an uncommon sight in those rebellious days in Roman provinces. The cross was the worst instrument of capital punishment known to Roman law. It was one of those things the Romans held up before the people as a constant reminder this would be their fate if they did anything against Rome. Crucifixions were always conducted in a public place.

It is said that one time Napoleon, along with his advisors, spread out a large map of the continent of Europe. He methodically traced the various nations. Moving his hand over what we now know as Great Britain, he said, "If it were not for that spot, I could conquer the world!" He recognized that Britain could keep him from his goal forever.

Surely Satan looks at this world and says that without the cross of Calvary he would have free reign, he could conquer the world! But Jesus' cross makes all the difference!

The two men crucified along with Jesus had great physiques and had not failed to carry their crosses on the journey to the hill. But neither had they been beaten with thirty-nine stripes the night before, which was often enough to kill a man.

The journey was completed and the crosses put in place. It seemed the end of everything for this Galilean on the center cross. The two thieves hung, one on one side and one on the other. The Bible does not name them. Tradition, however, gives each of them a name. The repentant one has been called Dismas, the unrepentant one, Gestas. These two recognized their guilt and why they were there. They had known for some days that they would be tried and likely crucified. But it was surprising that Barabbas, who had been among them and had suffered their common lot in jail, was not on the third cross.

They looked at this man in the middle curiously. One of them, evidently not knowing Jesus, may have heard tales of this reputed prophet. Rumors of his ministry might have penetrated even the jail. Maybe they heard the excitement of Jerusalem on Palm Sunday, when Jesus rode into the city in a cheering throng. Seemingly without any reason, one of the thieves turned and railed on Jesus. Why? What did Jesus have to do with his being on the cross? Jesus wasn't at his trial.

Perhaps he merely picked up the mockery of the rulers of the Jews who taunted Jesus: "He saved others; let him save himself, if he be Christ, the chosen of God," and the soldiers, who said, "If thou be the king of the Jews, save thyself." (Luke 23:35,37). They dared him to come down from the cross.

Rejection

There was moral blackness around that cross, because the thief's hatred was turned against an innocent man in utter rejection. It was an apparent attempt to humiliate Jesus further in front of the crowd.

He turned against Jesus, saying, "If thou be Christ, save thyself and us!" (Luke 23:39). Had he said what he really meant, he would have said, "Save me, and save yourself if you can!"

These three crosses looked the same, but how vastly different the attitudes of the men. Hatred destroys. It can turn a man against the innocent. It can cause people to strike out against those who never lifted a hand against them in wrong. Why did Gestas speak against Christ? Could he have been envious? Was he a man who flexed his mucles and prided himself on being strong?

On the center cross hung a man who had collapsed under the weight of his cross, yet now seemed completely in control of himself. He did not even seem to fear death. Was the unrepentant thief envious of this one who had no fear of what Rome could do to him?

It took a little effort for Gestas to utter his anger. In crucifixion, the men did not die from loss of blood. Really, they died of self-strangulation. They had difficulty in holding themselves up. When the pain became unbearable and the desire to breathe was greater than any pain, a gasp for breath pulled the feet and hands against the cruel nails. Between desperate, painful gasps, this man, in his torture and suffering, turned in hate against the only one who could have helped him.

It is strange why people turn against those who try to help them. But Gestas is a symbol of them. He was so near Christ, just as near as the other cross. He could have gained forgiveness and a promise of Paradise as did the other thief. But he died in sin and hatred, tortured and without hope. There was desperation in his words, of course. He was dying in total despair.

"Now it is perfectly true that the thief who was lost addressed the Lord as Christ. But he made a fatal mistake. He made the mistake of prefacing that Name with a little word of two letters— 'if.' 'If,' he said, 'thou be Christ.' 'If'—and so that man was lost." [1]

Repentance

Defense often comes from unexpected sources. Dismas was the thief on the other side of Jesus who demonstrated repentance. Between his heaves and gasps, this suffering man did not speak to Jesus immediately. Rather, he turned to his fellow thief, as far as he could turn his head, and said, "Dost thou not fear God, seeing thou art in the same condemnation? And we indeed justly; for we receive the due reward of our deeds: but this man hath done nothing amiss" (Luke 23:40–41).

Spiritually, this cross glows golden with repentance and remission. His knowledge was limited, but his prayer came straight from his heart.

This one was as guilty of crimes against humanity and the law as the other thief, yet he had a different attitude. He turned to the suffering Lord in his desperation. He evidently reasoned, "What have I got to lose?"

Dismas turned to Jesus and reached out in hope. "Lord, remember me, when thou comest into thy kingdom," was his sincere request.

In genuine, heartfelt repentance, he admitted he was due the reward of death on the cross. He claimed no merit whatsoever. He did not plead, "I am innocent." He had no time for pretense. Life was fast ebbing away.

Luke is the only Gospel that mentions this story of repentance. Even in his dying hour, anyone who turns to Jesus, God will save to the uttermost. The thief could not buy grace; he could not offer a sacrifice; he could not do a single good deed! Only, "Nothing in my hand I bring. Simply to Thy cross I cling!"

Every sinner is in that same desperate, hopeless condition.

One of our missionaries shares the story that many years ago an Indian chief in the western stated tried to buy a ticket on a train.

He was used to bartering with beads, and he tried to buy the ticket with them. They were not acceptable to the railroad and the chief angrily declared, "I am the richest man in my tribe!"

The problem was, he was out of the realm of his tribe and in another world. What he had to barter there was of no value.

It is true of us, also. We don't have anything of value with which to buy eternal life. The rich young ruler discovered this truth. We live in a physical world, and you don't buy spiritual things with material things. Salvation is God's gift. When the dying thief cried out, "Remember me!" Jesus gave his eternal "Yes!"

The Philadelphia Bulletin reported that a young man was involved in a brawl in which the matron of Haverford College was killed. He was sentenced to death for the crime. While in jail, he was saved and became a consecrated Christian. Having a good tenor voice, he also took an interest in sacred music. His favorite selection was, "No One Ever Cared for Me Like Jesus."

Just before he went to the electric chair, he spoke to the other prisoners in the exercise yard, telling them of his joy in the Lord. Concluding his testimony, he rendered his favorite hymn with deep feeling.

He sang it again all the way from death row to the electric chair. As the black hood was pulled down over his head, his last audible words were, "Till someday I see His blessed face above!"

Reconciliation

Look at the man on the middle cross. By most of the onlookers he was pronounced guilty by association as well. Look at him, he is with the common lot! Was it an accident he was not on the outside but right in the very middle?

But this was the only cross ever of hope and love. The cross of reconciliation and redemption is the hope of our salvation. Jesus was the Promised One. As he died there, the veil of the Temple in Jerusalem was torn from top to bottom. God's Lamb was forever slain.

Jesus said to the thief in words he could understand, "This day thou shalt be with me in paradise." Of Persian origin, "paradise" was a common word. Originally, it meant a walled garden, such as only kings had in the midst of that desert world. It was a great honor for the king to invite someone into his walled garden, out of the heat of the desert into a cool oasis. No one could enter except by such an invitation. To see trees, plants, water, and shade was paradise indeed! The rabbis of Jesus' day said that heaven was like that. An entrance was possible only by God's invitation.

Jesus turned to that dying thief and said to him, "Today shalt thou be with me in paradise" (Luke 23:43).

"Father, into thy hands I commend my spirit," Jesus said and died. The thief died also. The body of the thief was probably buried in a hastily-dug, unmarked trench, if at all. Loving friends buried the body of Jesus in a rich man's tomb-cave. Yet according to Jesus' promise, they were together—in the garden of God.

The Sunday School Times related the story of a mountain climbing party in the Alps. They came to a chasm where the only way to get across was for each climber in turn to place his foot in the outstretched hands of the guide who was a little way ahead. One man hesitated a moment as he looked into the depths below where he might fall to his death if anything went wrong.

"Have no fear, sir," the guide said. "In all my years of service my hands have never yet lost a man!"

There were originally three crosses and two thieves. One pictured rejection. One pictured repentance. The third held our sin and redemption, as God died there for us!

NOTES

1. F. E. Gaebelein, *Looking unto Him* (Grand Rapids: Zondervan Publishing House, 1941), p. 189.

11
JOHN
. . . who loved Him

Standing by the Savior
John 19:25–27

John, "the beloved disciple," does not use his own name to refer to himself in his Gospel. From the other Gospel writers we learn that "the disciple whom Jesus loved" was John, the son of Zebedee. His claim was not a brag, it was a joy. Jesus had given him this title and he bore it with gladness. It brought out the best in him.

Some labels we attach to people are not helpful, but others bring out the best in them.

A little fellow can usually bring out the best in a man by saying, in the right tone and the right way, "Father."

People can bring out whatever I might have within me when they call me "Pastor."

Jesus looked at John and called him the disciple whom he loved. John never forgot it! If Jesus was willing to refer to it, then he was willing to use that title with a sense of possession.

Three or four women stood by the cross. Only one man! That is, regrettably, about the percentage all through the ages—one man to four women who are active in the church, who carry the responsibilities of Christianity. This is tragic, but true.

Jesus' other disciples did not have any greater responsibility, and surely no more courage—they should not have been any less faith-

ful than these women. But while the disciples were excusing themselves, the women did the dangerous and difficult thing. They
followed Christ to Golgotha. Their hearts drew them and they
were there.

John was there because he could be no other place. Where else
could he possibly be? He loved Jesus and Jesus loved him. Jesus
was his friend, his Master. He had to be there with him.

Look at this apostle a moment. He wrote five books of the New
Testament—the Gospel of John, three epistles and the book of
Revelation. He only mentioned himself five times. All these are in
Revelation, where he had to refer to a personal experience.

In the Gospel, he called himself "that apostle whom Jesus
loved." But in the book of the Revelation, written in isolation on
Patmos, God was speaking to him and through him. There was
no other name he could use.

But John was not without fault. Surely he never forgot the
rebuke Jesus gave him and his brother, and their mother, when
they asked for positions of preferment. Evidently they already felt
themselves favorites.

James and John took Jesus aside and asked if they could sit with
him in his kingdom on his right hand and left hand.

"Ye know not what ye ask," Jesus replied. Did they have the
courage to face what he faced?

They insisted that they did. Jesus assured them that they would
have a chance to prove it. But positions in the kingdom were not
his to give.

Most of the Gospel of John concerns the last days of Jesus'
life—particularly the last twenty days. Ten chapters describe the
last week and last hours of Jesus' life. If there was anything John
the beloved wanted to leave in our minds it was that Jesus was the
Son of God, and that this Son of God loved us. One evidence of
this was his personal testimony—that Jesus loved even him!

Herschel Hobbs has said, concerning the Gospel of John, that it is the richest unveiling of Christ that we have. This says much concerning its writer, John. We probably read the Gospel of John more than any other because it tells us about the nature and love of Jesus Christ. This vision we always need desperately.

John wasn't always "the beloved." First of all, he was a fisherman. He was thought to be the youngest of the group of apostles. His older brother James was also one of the twelve, and they were the sons of Zebedee and Salome. The father was probably a very prosperous fisherman, as business went.

The brothers were busy about their nets when Jesus called them to follow him. Jesus never called a man that wasn't doing something, and he never will. If you cannot find something to do for your family and for society, you are not going to find anything to do for God.

Self-Surrender

Jesus came by, looked at James and John and saw in them great potential. "Follow me!" he said. So began John's self-surrender. Just following Jesus step by step, day by day, instead of fishing, was not the only decision he had to make. There was self-will involved.

The hot-blooded young John and his brother once urged Jesus to call down fire on an unfriendly village (Luke 9:54). Jesus called them "the sons of thunder." That is, they could square off at each other with the slightest provocation. They were rash. They had a temper. They were not always considerate. They made demands. They seemed to have been raised in that kind of climate.

Some psychologists make much about the weaknesses and strengths that we inherit. Parents, particularly, need to be more conscious of the fact that what we inherit is not nearly such a problem as the climate of the home which a child absorbs after he is born. What they catch, what they observe, what they hear! If the parents are always thundering about everything that comes up, the children will likely follow the same pattern—or go to the far extreme and be noncommittal about everything.

If the children have "roast preacher" for dinner, they are not likely to grow into a dedicated life. They catch more than they inherit.

Salome, the mother of James and John, came to Jesus with the same ambitious request as her sons. "I want my sons to be able to sit on your right and your left in your kingdom!" Every mother should aspire, but there is a difference between praying for God to use your child in the will of God for their lives—and demanding, pushing, prodding them to achieve popularity and shoving them ahead at the expense of all others.

The family of Zebedee hadn't understood that service and love make a person great, not merely an elected office. Even if Jesus had appointed James and John number one and number two, they still wouldn't have *been* number one and number two among the others unless they earned it.

In many ways, John did earn the position of number one by always being there to help, by his art of standing by. He was called a "son of thunder," yet he was among the three closed confidantes of Jesus.

No man learns the art of standing by until he learns something of self-surrender. Thus John gave up his tendency to angry, crude, and personal demands, his thunderous tones. He came to his last days speaking more of love than any one else in the Scriptures.

Substitute Son

At the cross, there was John, standing by! What could he do? For a man to feel helpless is perhaps one of the most difficult things imaginable. If you could just do something! If you could just help!

If you could just change things—grab it with your hands and shake it—or if you could say the word and do it! But John did something for Jesus, though we have no record of words spoken by John to Jesus. Because he was just *there*.

Jesus was dying. He looked around at the hostile crowd. He looked at John, his "beloved disciple," standing by and said, "Son, behold thy mother!" In a ceremony performed by Jesus from the cross, he formally made John the substitute son of Mary his mother.

There was not time to discuss why the Master did not choose one of his younger half-brothers, James or Jude. The legal ceremony of the Jewish marriage contract was, "Behold the woman! —Behold the man!" Jesus was saying, "John, behold thy mother." And to his mother, "Behold thy son." Jesus knew that he could depend upon John.

We learn through sickness, through sorrow, through life itself. When things go wrong, when things go right, through tears and joys! We learn who stands by and who we can depend on. Some men will always be remembered because they stood by the church through thick and thin. Or they stood by their children through thick and thin.

E. S. James is to me one of the greatest living men. When he was a pastor, he helped me in a revival meeting in a former pastorate. His son was away in summer school but called and asked his father if he could come over. He did. I gave Dr. James as much free time that day as possible. But the son was just there with him. That night after the service, the boy made a long drive back to school.

Dr. James was deeply touched. "I'd rather have had my son with me today," he told me," just being here when he didn't have to, just standing by me, just coming to hear me preach, than anything he could ever do for me!"

He added that he had told his children if they would tell him the truth, it didn't matter what they did, he would stand by them through hell if he had to—just as long as they would tell him the truth. The reason that boy wanted to stand by his father was that he had seen his father stand by for a lifetime—always ready!

Jesus, who knew all things, knew that John loved him and would look after Mary, his mother, for the sake of that love. Love carries its responsibilities. You can't love without caring for. John became the substitute son.

Spiritual Symbol

John also became a spiritual symbol. He was changed from a "son of thunder" to an exponent of Christian love. His often-used phrase, "Love one another!" revealed how much he had become a new creature. Surely John is also a spiritual symbol of what can happen to a life surrendered to Christ.

This is the whole point of Christianity—what conversion is all about. John became the apostle of sympathy, compassion and love.

In Galatians 2:9, Paul pictures John as a pillar in the early church: "And when James, Cephas [Peter], and John, who seemed to be pillars, perceived the grace that was given unto me, they gave to me and Barnabas the right hands of fellowship."

John penned perhaps our greatest New Testament verse: "God so loved the world, that he gave his only begotten Son, that whosoever believeth in him should not perish, but have everlasting life" (John 3:16).

He mentioned love fifty times in his writings. In his old age, when people came to him with their problems, he would say, "Love one another!" This is the best counsel you can give your children, your church, your class, your neighbor, your friends—love one another!

John was not speaking to babies when he exhorted them, "Little children, love one another."

According to the words of John, "Jesus gives a simple test by which his disciples can be recognized," said Samuel J. Schreiner. " 'A new commandment I give unto you. That ye love one another.' . . . In writing his letter to the early Christians, John elaborated on this test—'This is his commandment, That we should believe on the name of his Son Jesus Christ, and love one another, as he gave us commandment' (1 John 3:23–24). Again John says, 'By this it may be seen who are the children of God— whosoever does not do right is not of God, nor he who does not love the brethren.'

"Love then, even toward the unlovely, is the characteristic mark of a Christian. Jesus gives us a clue as to how they can be recognized: 'By their fruits you shall know them.' " [1]

John lived to be a great old patriarch. He may have been the only apostle that didn't die a martyr's death.

He is a symbol of worship, telling us as much about worship as anyone in the New Testament. On Patmos, he seems to have had a spiritual experience something like Isaiah had in the sixth chapter, "I saw the Lord, high and lifted up!"

John's words from Patmos picture the sufficiency of Christ even in isolation: "I was in the Spirit on the Lord's day!" (Rev. 1:10).

If only we could understand how necessary it is to participate in corporate worship, to be in God's house at God's appointed time. John was isolated. He didn't have a soul there with him, yet on the Lord's Day he had a worship service—just him and God!

In fact, if you do not have a relationship with God in any church service, you really haven't worshiped, you have just attended. Some people do not get anything out of church because they do not lift their hearts up to God before they look around. The test of a man's genuineness of devotion to God is, If you were the only man on earth, would you still worship him? Would you still recognize the Lord's Day? John did.

This great apostle, once ambitious, selfish, and angry, came to a time in life when he no longer followed his own way, but the Master's way of love. He went on "standing by." Standing by the cross, if there was anything he could do for Jesus. Standing by Jesus' mother, if there was anything he could do for her. Standing by the church at Ephesus if there was anything he could do for them.

And his message to all was, Love one another!

NOTES

1. William S. Cannon, compiler, *Every Day Five Minutes with God* (Nashville: Broadman Press, 1969), p. 157.

12
THE CENTURION
. . . who confessed Him

An Unexpected Declaration
Matthew 27:50–54

The people around the cross were operating in the present tense. They were making instant judgment. Two thousand years later we are making judgment in the light of history.

We have been viewing the cross from the eyes of those who watched Jesus Christ die there. We considered those who had a part in condemning Jesus: the high priests, Judas, Pilate, and the crowd. Now we turn to the confessions that came as a result of the death of Jesus. First, we have the confession of a Roman centurion and then the belated confessions of Nicodemus and Joseph of Arimathaea.

It is being said in many quarters that only the friends of Jesus had anything to say on his behalf. The records of Jesus written by his friends naturally gave a kind interpretation. There are others who insist that the close friends of Jesus actually stole his body away. As we consider all the personalities around the cross, one of the most forceful statements came from one who was not a believer. Up to this time, he evidently had no association with Jesus at all.

The enemies of Jesus were indeed prejudiced witnesses. But there were those by the cross without any intention of considering

Jesus as the Son of God. They were there on the job, doing their professional duty without any personal interest whatever.

The centurion, certainly, was there in the line of duty. He surely cannot be classified as a disciple, follower, or friend. He represented all Rome stood for and was entrusted with great responsibility. He had no genuine interest in Jesus or his religion. The soldiers of Rome had seen many religions and they had many gods of their own. Indeed, each new Caesar was a new god for them.

The task of crucifying men was this centurion's assigned duty, and he was proficient at it. He had come to the place where he could do his job without much personal emotion. When he left the barracks that morning with the group of soldiers under his command, he did not think the crucifixion of these three men would make this day different from any of the others.

According to the military system, a centurion ranked as a high noncommissioned officer. He had under his command about a hundred soldiers. Probably he only took a detachment with him that day. But he had total responsibility as Rome's representative. The centurion had to carry out the orders of Rome regardless of what those orders might require.

That this man would say a good word for Jesus is rather strange. But always it is in mysterious ways that God performs his miracles.

There are at least four centurions in God's Word who are mentioned favorably concerning the things of God.

The name of Cornelius comes to mind. The Bible says he was a just man, a good man, one who gave offerings to God and prayed. In Acts, we have the story of how he sent for Simon Peter to come to his house. "We are all here present before God," Cornelius told Peter, "to hear all things that are commanded thee of God" (Acts 10:33).

Then there is another, unnamed centurion who gave the money to build a synagogue in Capernaum. A centurion usually had a share of the spoils of war. Often centurions became very wealthy men. Therefore some would try to atone for their lives by good deeds such as giving to religious causes.

A centurion by the name of Julius was in charge of the apostle Paul on his trip to Rome as a prisoner (Acts 27:1–3). This man treated Paul kindly, and every word Paul spoke of him showed high regard for this Roman soldier.

The fourth centurion stood beneath the cross of Jesus. We do not know his name, though tradition calls him Marcellus. About seven hours at the most was all the occasion this man had to be acquainted with Jesus of Nazareth.

On that day before the Jewish Passover, Marcellus and his men took Jesus and two other prisoners to the hill called Golgotha. The crucifying of Jesus and the two thieves was a murderous business. Many had died by the Romans' swords, and they had lost sensitivity to seeing people suffer. To the soldiers it was nothing more than a routine job to be done as quickly as possible.

Although calloused by death, this Roman soldier was sensitive to the difference in Jesus. As Jesus died, the centurion exclaimed, "Truly this was the Son of God" (Matt. 27:54).

On what basis? It was an unusual statement for a Roman soldier to make.

Wondering Witness

There were several factors. One, because of the manner of Jesus' suffering, of which this man was a wondering witness.

The centurion had seen many people suffer. This was not uncommon to his job. He had seen many men die—but not with peace of mind or feeling of accomplishment in life. To him, the proof of courage was not what men bragged about in life, but how they died. Perhaps this was because he usually saw them only in their dying hours.

This soldier was not used to observing men's lives. Rather, he was used to observing their deaths. He had not seen one die with such boldness, such courage, and such quietness. Some dying men cursed everybody in sight. Some bragged about their accomplishments. Some claimed innocence. Some declared they were not afraid of anything, but when death came they were scared, nevertheless.

A chaplain visited the hospital room of a man who could cuss in a very colorful manner, hiding his weakness under profane language. When there was no one in the room except the two he said quietly, "Chaplain, to tell you the truth, I'm scared to death!" The centurion had seen men who were scared to death.

He had seen them bold and cursing, protesting loudly. He had watched them as his subordinates stripped them. But Jesus offered no resistance. Even though "he could have called ten thousand angels!"

Wonderful Words

The centurion was impressed not only by the manner in which Jesus suffered, but because of his wondeful words, as well. There were two others being crucified, one on each side. The contrast of the words of the man on the right and left was startling in comparison to the words of Jesus.

Jesus spoke seven times from the cross. Perhaps the centurion moved up closer to Jesus because of his quietness, observing him. Surely he wondered about the strange statement: "Father forgive them!" Jesus could have been looking into the eyes of the centurion when he said it. "Forgive them, for they know not what they do!" Jesus prayed. This must have struck home to the soldier's hardened heart.

Even in Jesus' dying moment he was thinking about those around him—the thieves, the soldiers, his mother, and his disciples. He said nothing concerning his own pain. He turned away offer of the dulling drug. He was alert to the very last.

What more did Jesus say? He quoted the twenty-second Psalm, "Why hast thou forsaken me?" And finally, "Father, into thy hands I commend my spirit!" No wonder the centurion was attracted to Jesus because of his words.

Wavering World

But far more violent than Jesus' words and actions were the dramatic natural manifestations of the hour—a wavering world. The centurion was attracted to this strange man on the cross because of the reaction of the whole earth. It seemed to him this was the first time that the earth had ever taken notice of a man's death. It seemed as if light died. The sun went down at noonday. The earth quivered and shook as if caught in death throes. Darkness dropped like a curtain for three hours. The centurion had to stay the whole time.

This was not an ordinary eclipse of the sun. It was total darkness, the kind that paralyzes men. Sinister, threatening, with no apparent explanation. Some of the people said that surely some god must be dying. They did not recognize that in truth the Son of God *was* dying. This was the blackness of sin without the light of the Savior.

A startling event happened in Jerusalem at the same time. The great veil of the Temple was rent in twain, that is, torn in two from top to bottom. It is estimated that it would take the strength of forty teams of oxen to pull this thick embroidered curtain apart. It was heavy tapestry, strongly woven, made exclusively for the separation between the holy of holies and the holy place of the Temple. It may have been two or three inches thick. For it to tear was unbelievable! Some said an earthquake. Others knew it to be an act of God.

Behind this curtain only the high priest was allowed to in once a year. The day Jesus died, God ripped it open with unseen hands so that through Christ's death everyone might have access to God's mercy seat.

Thirdly, the rocks fell from the hillsides and the whole earth trembled at the exact time Jesus gave up his spirit, and many graves nearby opened of themselves.

After the resurrection of Jesus, some who had been buried came out of the graves and went into Jerusalem. Their testimony was added to the testimony of Lazarus, and it is hard to deny the testimony of dead men.

The centurion, after witnessing all of this, exclaimed, "Surely this must have been the Son of God!"

Already we know this Roman was not a man given to emotional thinking. He was a man of rationalization. But emotion has something to do with intellect. You cannot make an intellectual decision about Jesus Christ without making an emotional decision. Pilate made an intellectual decision, based on his own selfish interests.

The centurion's startling statement was based on reality and truth as he saw it. The decisions of these two men in the employ of Rome were vastly opposite. Pilate sentenced Jesus, but the centurion judged him with an honest and open mind. He made a historical statement rather than expressing faith in the Son of God.

"He must be the Son of God!"

Lew Wallace, an unbeliever at the time, once was talking with Robert Ingersol, a noted atheist who attacked Christianity.

"I am going to read the New Testament and find out for myself," Lew Wallace declared. For six years he studied it carefully. Then he wrote the famous novel, *Ben Hur.* His personal testimony was, "After thoroughly studying the sacred Scriptures, I have come to the conviction that Jesus Christ is the Messiah of the Jews, the Savior of the world, and my own personal Redeemer."

13
THE MARYS
. . . who mourned Him

The Faithful Few
Mark 15:39–41

There was a group of women on the road to Golgotha, the women of Jerusalem. This is the only time they are identified. Another group of women gathered close to the foot of the cross. We remember these as the women who mourned Jesus.

In the New Testament, six Marys are mentioned—the name occurring fifty-one times. Of these, fifty are related to five women, the fifty-first to a sixth, the one whom we think of as Mary of Rome, mentioned only once (Rom. 16:6).

John Mark's mother can be referred to as Mary of Jerusalem. Then there was Mary the wife of Cleopas, and Mary Magdalene. And Mary the mother of Jesus.

Even though the name Mary does not appear in the Old Testament, the Hebrew name from which it is derived, Miriam, appeared many times. We are told that there are at least seventy meanings or interpretation of what that name meant in various generations as it has been passed down.

Which of these six Marys were at the cross? Not Mary of Rome, certainly. Mary the mother of Jesus was there. And "Mary, the mother of James the less and of Joses"—that is, the wife of Alphaeus. Mary Magdalene, definitely. She became one of the really great women of the New Testament.

Not all the Marys were with Jesus when he died. Now, "many other women" (Mark 15:41) with Jesus is an inclusive term. We cannot be positive who all these unnamed women were.

It seems strange that the sister of Martha and Lazarus is not found in any of the Gospel accounts as being present when Jesus died, although providentially she anointed Jesus beforehand for his burial. However, she is not found in that small group who stood off from the cross and mourned Jesus.

There were others than Marys who were there. For instance, Salome. Evidently the men had already left. John is the only one we know as a follower of Christ who stood nearby.

Four women and one man—the faithful few! The percentage is about the same now. Women can be counted on in difficult times when others turn aside and go their self-appointed ways.

Why did this group stand "afar off"? The expression "looking on afar off" (Mark 15:40) should not leave the impression that they were cowardly, or that they felt any personal danger. They may have been closer during the earlier stages of the crucifixion. The account covers a six-hour period. Perhaps, out of reverence and respect, when in humiliating Jesus they stripped the robe from him, the women moved to a greater distance.

During the intensity of his suffering and the death watch, maybe the other women carefully, lovingly, moved Mary, Jesus' mother, a little farther away from the agony of the cross. They may have stood around her and encircled her. There was nothing cowardly about their actions at all. They were there.

These women loved him and followed him. The Bible says they came up to Jerusalem with him. They stayed with him until the end. The disciples' inner circle is mentioned. This seems to be the inner circle of the women who followed our Lord. It wasn't easy to see their beloved Master suffer. Yet they were there.

Were they there for their own hearts' sake? Were they there for his mother's sake? Were they there for Jesus' sake? Or were they just there and didn't quite understand why? That is very possible. Only those who held him dearest endured the dreadful scene.

Mary, Who Was Forgiven

Look first at Mary Magdalene, who was forgiven by Jesus. Every one of the Gospel writers mentioned that she was at the cross. They not only place her at the scene itself, but at the tomb, later, watching Joseph and Nicodemus preparing the body for burial. Anything that she could do, she did.

She also came early in the morning to the grave. She was not expecting a resurrection, so why did she go out there that morning? It was a practical reason. Jesus had been buried hurriedly, late in the evening, and there was not time for them fully to prepare the body in the Jewish tradition.

Therefore she and the other women, as soon as they could after the sabbath, went to further embalm the body, more than the wrapping with "mixture of myrrh and aloes, about an hundred pound weight" which Nicodemus had provided.

Really, we know little about Mary Magdalene. Yet she is identified very often in the Scriptures. The word "Magdalene" refers to the town from which she came, just as the word "Nazarene" referred to where Jesus grew up. She was a true convert. One with a past. And yet we do not know about this. One of the Gospel writers referred to her as the woman out of whom the Lord had cast seven demons.

Seven deadly sins have been catalogued. Some of the great theologicans feel that perhaps she was guilty of all seven, which Jesus referred to as "seven demons."

After Jesus died, some of the disciples went back to fishing, and some of them just turned back. But Mary could never forget, even in the midst of his apparent failure to achieve his purposes. To many of his followers it seemed that he had promised much and delivered nothing. He did not rise to the challenge of coming down from the cross and saving himself and them—it seemed. He died and soon would be forgotten. His friends would be sought out for arrest and questioning. So they thought—and disappeared.

Mary did not think of him as a failure, as did others. She recognized in herself a great change. Indeed, he had made of her a new creature. She was a different woman. She dared to think of herself as a lady. Jesus always referred to her as one. She couldn't forget that! Whether he was a failure or not never crossed Mary Magdalene's mind. Because he had made her something, he was much. She didn't debate it, nor did she understand. She just stayed.

She received a great reward for staying and for being eager to serve by going to the tomb that first day of the week. She was the first of the New Testament Christians to be told of Jesus' resurrection and to see the risen Savior. What a reward! She was the first one commanded to tell the story that the tomb was empty. "He is not here, but is risen!" (Luke 24:6).

Mary Magdalene did not know her coming reward when she was enduring the cross, any more than we know God's reward, generosity, and mercy for us when we stand near the cross. No service for our Lord goes unnoticed by him.

Mary, Who Was Faithful

There was another Mary, who was faithful in standing by. She is mentioned four times in the Gospels, usually as the mother of James the Less and Joses. She is believed by some to be the wife of Cleopas, the one on the Emmaus Road (but "James the Less" is called the son of Alphaeus in Matt. 10:3).

This Mary has often been confused with others. The Roman Catholics believe her to be a sister of Mary the mother of Jesus.

Not many Protestant scholars accept this. If she were the sister of Jesus' mother, there would be the problem of two Marys in the same family. The New Testament doesn't put emphasis on family relationships. Jesus said, "Who is my mother and my brothers?" The emphasis was not upon kinship, but upon spiritual relationship to Jesus. More than just family ties kept these women at the cross.

The Gospels sufficiently identify this Mary as one who stood by the cross of Jesus. That is quite an epitaph! That is the way to be remembered—not by your husband's name, not by your children's names, but in your own right to be listed as one who stood by the cross of Jesus.

She also became a witness to the empty tomb. She was one of the three who went there to anoint his body. But she did not spend her time staying at the cross and grieving her life away; she did not even spend her time staying at the empty tomb, glorious as that was.

We see this Mary, in latter years, identified with the church of Jesus Christ. There are some who will stand by when the times are unusual. There are others who will stay in the glorious times when heaven comes down and glory fills our souls. But we need more who will stand by and be a part of the church of the living God the rest of their days. This Mary did.

Salome, Who Sought Fame

Salome also was there by the cross. She stood with the other women afar off. Bear in mind that the distance may have varied over the hours. They must have been within speaking distance, because in his last hours Jesus said, "Woman, behold thy son." They were close enough for John to hear the words of Jesus, "Behold thy mother." We cannot be sure when they moved away from that agony, that erect deathbed, the shameful last scenes, away into the distance. But it was a kind distance.

Geographical distance made no difference in their hearts. It did not mean far away—a far country, as in the parable of the prodigal son.

Salome beheld Jesus die, but she also beheld the empty tomb. She heard the glorious message of the angel. Her greatest fame had been as the mother of James and John. Some time earlier she had made an unwise request on their behalf and been rebuked by Jesus. "Grant that these my two sons," she said, "may sit, the one on thy right hand, and the other on the left, in thy kingdom" (Matt. 20:21).

"Ye know not what ye ask," Jesus replied. She didn't recognize it, but Jesus was already moving in the kingdom of God, and indeed James and John were of the inner circle.

The rebuke was because she was interested in the prominence of her sons rather than the glory of Jesus. She wanted her sons to be recognized along with the Master. When one used Jesus' name, obviously the next thought would be of James and John. They just belonged with him. We do belong with him . . . not out of a sense of prominence, but rather out of a sense of service.

The wife of Zebedee did her best for her children. She even wanted some things that were not best for them. But before we rebuke this woman, we need to remember that we have wished for things just as unwise—but perhaps more carefully worded, or more wisely left unsaid.

Someone has well said that the child who disobeys his parents will be likely also to disobey God. There was not much written about Zebedee in the early life of James and John, but there must have been something about the devotion in this home that tied it together and prepared these sons for the Lord's use.

Mary, Who Was Favored Among Women

Why didn't we mention first the name of Mary, the mother of

Jesus? We saved her until the last: Mary of Nazareth, who was favored among women.

All the Gospels acknowledge her presence at the cross. She was preeminently the mourning mother. She was there because she could be nowhere else. Her heart made her come . . . and stay to the end.

Surely she remembered some of the words prophesied to her many years before, when he was a baby. "A sword shall pierce through thy own soul also" (Luke 2:35). She witnessed that lance open the side of Jesus. It was like opening a wound in her own heart.

> And Mary stood beside the cross! Her soul
> Pierced with the selfsame wound that rent His side
> Who hung thereon. She watched Him as He died—
> Her son! Saw Him paying the cruel toll
> Exacted by the law, and unbelief,
> Since He their evil will had dared defy.
> There stood the mother helpless in her grief,
> Beside the cross, and saw her firstborn die!
>
> —CLYDE MCGEE [1]

Some have made far too much of Mary, especially in calling her sinless. They would make her the mother of Jesus only—having no other children. They would make her the mediator between man and Jesus. Yet the veil of the Temple was rent from top to bottom so that there would be no barrier of any kind between us and God.

We have to admit that we usually have not thought enough about the mother of Jesus, and all that her privilege and position meant.

This was not the first time Mary had suffered. She endured the gossip of neighbors before her belated marriage to Joseph. She was the mother of one of whom it was said, "Can any good come out of Nazareth?"

Mary had the same problem with Jesus, the Son of God, that every mother has—the difficulty of being able to turn loose and let go. At the wedding in Cana of Galilee, she suggested how he was to conduct himself and he had to speak to her bluntly. Mary pondered those things in her heart.

She came to the cross a faithful, godly mother, suffering as much as any other mother could suffer at the death of her child. And even more so because of his innocence.

No word is written of what these women said, standing near the cross. There was no response, apparently, on the par of Mary or any of the others to the statements Jesus made that pertained most to them. And yet, how her soul must have ached! How her heart seemed to stand still! How distressed she was! She did not understand the nature and the will of God when the child was born. Nor did she understand any better, watching him on the cross, pondering why her holy son had to suffer. Certainly she was far more concerned about his suffering than she was about any pain that came to her because of him.

We do not hear the end of Mary of Nazareth at the cross. In Acts, she is mentioned as part of the community of Christians. She did not say: "I have done my bit, I have served, now I can quit!" Wherever Christians met to worship God, she was there.

Others, Who Were Fearful

Can we fully comprehend and communicate with the hearts of the many others mentioned in Mark 15:41? Who were they? Why were they there? From whence did they come? What happened to them? They represent all Christian women—perhaps unnamed, who were fearful but not unconcerned. Their epitaphs are written in the words, "And they stood by the cross." You are one of those women if you can be counted on to stand by.

Only a faithful few, but what solace to the suffering Savior!

Although he had been betrayed, denied, sold out, and crucified, he was not forgotten.

He was not unmindful of the men who had departed for the sake of their own hides. Neither was he unmindful of the fact that these women would always be there when the church met. This was the beginning of a multitude of faithful Christian women through the centuries.

And, thank God, they still stand by . . . and will till Jesus comes!

NOTES

1. James Dalton Morrison, ed., *Masterpieces of Religious Verse* (New York and London: Harper and Brothers, 1948).

14
SECRET DISCIPLES
. . . who buried Him

The Prolonged Confession
John 19:38–42

The term "secret discipleship" is in itself a contradiction. How can this be? Discipleship doesn't remain secret. The two wealthy and educated men, Joseph of Arimathaea and Nicodemus, came into the open when they asked Pilate for the body of Jesus that they might honorably bury him.

Joseph of Arimathaea, until he heard the claims of Christ, seems to have been a contented man in a small Jewish city. He evidently possessed material things in abundance.

Nicodemus also had a high station in life. He was well educated, a leader, a teacher of the Law. Yet evidently each of these men felt a lack of perfect peace and ease of mind. As philosophers would search, they were searching.

From the situation in which we find these men later on, we can draw certain conclusions. Were there times when Joseph and Nicodemus wished they had never heard of Jesus? After his death, this had passed.

We meet these men, as disciples, after Jesus died on the cross. But they must have been there.

Nicodemus sat at the feet of the Master-teacher, coming to him by night in secrecy, early in the ministry of Jesus. Jesus' words must have disturbed him, perhaps they precipitated a continual inner battle, when he was trying to be on both sides at the same time. Pitiful is the person who tries to please everybody and have peace in his own mind as well. After Nicodemus had talked to Jesus and after Joseph had watched Jesus, these men could never have been content within themselves.

It may be that the disciples knew of their interest in Jesus. But they must have had doubts about Joseph and Nicodemus, as Christians did about Saul of Tarsus later. These men were members of the Sanhedrin and sat in the council of the high priest. Therefore surely the disciples raised barriers of prejudice to any claim of friendship on the part of Joseph and Nicodemus. In other words, the disciples had made clear-cut decisions, breaking with their old life. You either leave all, they reasoned—nets, law books, position, and the Sanhedrin—or you have no part with Jesus Christ.

Position

Look at the position of these men for a moment. They were men of wealth—at least Joseph was. Nicodemus seemed to have more in reputation and status than in material possessions.

However, to be members of the Sanhedrin, they had to be property owners and citizens of importance. These men stood tall among the most respectable of their people. Luke said Joseph was "a good man and a just" (Luke 23:50). These two adjectives give us an incisive picture of him. When you talk about someone being a good man, you are talking about his internal righteousness. "A just man" reflects his external conduct. Inside and out, the Gospel writer implied, Joseph was a superior man.

He was a watcher for the Messiah. He looked for the coming of the kingdom of God. He and Nicodemus were expecting the Messiah, but they were not sure that Jesus was the one.

If we had liberty of imagination, there are many things we could say about these men. We can call them brethren now. However, John stops short by saying they acted "secretly for fear of the Jews" (John 19:38). He didn't leave any doubt about it. They lacked courage because they feared the loss of their positions. Nicodemus, of course, would have to give up his teaching position in the rabbinical school.

Evidently they weighed one thing against another in their devotion to Jesus Christ. All men do this. We all weigh consequences and tend to choose a course of self-protection.

Peril

In the time of peril, these secret disciples stopped short of having courage. When they should have recognized the persecuted Christ as the Promised One of God, confessed him openly, and acknowledged him Lord of life, they lacked boldness.

Nicodemus is mentioned at least three times in the New Testament. In John 3 he is identified as one who sought Jesus by night. At that time, obviously, he didn't want people to know that he was interested in Jesus and what he had to say.

John also said that he spoke up for Jesus during his early ministry, when Jesus was accused before the Sanhedrin. "Nicodemus saith unto them, (he that came unto Jesus by night, being one of them,) Doth our law judge any man, before it hear him, and know what he doeth?" (John 7:50–51).

During all this time, nothing was said of Joseph. But the report was out that the Sanhedrin were consenting to Jesus' death. The disciples may well have been asking what happened to Jesus' "friends" in high places.

Let us presume here. Bear in mind that the Sanhedrin was called together unlawfully, in the wee hours of the night, in a totally unexpected move by the enemies of Jesus. It may have been that they did not have all members present, that they satisfied them-

selves with a quorum. It may have been that Joseph and Nicodemus, informed in the middle of the night, made a quick appraisal
of the situation. Recognizing that it was a life and death matter,
they chose not to appear. They were lacking in courage, protecting
themselves. They may have slept in, willfully missing the accusations by the high priest, Sadducees, and Pharisees. Some men
choose this course.

We all wish we could find some evidence in the record where
somebody spoke up for Jesus. Evidently nothing was said on Jesus'
behalf. Joseph and Nicodemus may have surmised that there was
no way to save him, nothing they could do—as the record gives
no defense. Nobody stood up and said, like Joshua of old, "As for
me and my house, we will serve the Lord!" (Josh. 24:15). Their
choice was quite the opposite in courage.

Jesus was very definite about the demands of discipleship.
"Whosoever therefore shall confess me before men, him will I
confess also before my Father which is in heaven. But whosoever
shall deny me before men, him will I also deny before my Father
which is in heaven" (Matt. 10:32–33). The Bible is positive and
without apology, then and now, concerning our affection to Christ.

Performance

Let's look at the performance of these men at the point of crisis.
What did it take for Joseph and Nicodemus finally to realize that
Jesus was the Messiah? Perhaps watching him die on the cross.
They had watched everything he did, maybe even sitting with the
Sanhedrin in that illegal, early-morning trial.

The Pharisees considered burial very important, as they believed
in the resurrection. The Sadducees did not. To the Pharisees, a
body should not be desecrated, but laid to rest as soon as possible.

It was the responsibility of the head of every Jewish household
to take care of the burial arrangements for his family. Joseph had

completed his own tomb, a grave in a garden, like a cave, a place large enough for all his family.

The tomb was very close to Calvary, we believe, where Jesus was crucified. Did Joseph offer it because of its closeness and convenience? No, I think he offered it because there was no other tomb in which to bury Jesus, and probably no one in the family of Jesus had money for his burial.

It was not unusual for a Jewish man to boast about his prepared burial place. It was something he always did in his lifetime. It was an evidence of his love for his family and his belief in the resurrection. It was something they were willing to talk about—unlike our concept of hushed tones today.

Joseph had no idea that he might be getting ready a tomb for the Son of God. The timing of God works in mysterious ways. Jesus, who was born of a virgin womb, was buried in a virgin tomb.

When Joseph learned that Jesus had been crucified, he took desperate courage and went to Pilate. Luke said that he begged for the body of Jesus—that is, he pleaded for it.

This would mean several changes in his life. For the rest of his days he would live under suspicion, both from Pilate and from the Sanhedrin. It was not unusual for the Sanhedrin to have spies in Pilate's court and elsewhere. They would know exactly what went on. Joseph was aware of that, but at long last he threw caution to the winds.

He did the bold thing! He couldn't stand for the body of Jesus to be treated as was the custom with those who had been crucified. Many times they were left on the cross until the cross was needed again. If they were buried at all, it was in a potter's field. The manner in which they were buried was a desecration to the Jewish concept.

Something reached down into the mind and heart of Joseph and gave him the courage to stand up and be counted. Evidently it took the death of Jesus for him to see his own heart.

When Joseph went to Pilate and asked for the body of Jesus, Pilate didn't then know that Jesus was dead. Usually a man who was crucified didn't die so quickly. When it was affirmed by the centurion that Jesus was already dead, Pilate did an unusual thing in consenting to let Joseph have the body of Jesus.

With the permission in his hand, bearing the seal of approval from Pilate, Joseph started toward the cross. Somewhere between Pilate's hall and Calvary's hill, he met Nicodemus.

Nicodemus went with Joseph the rest of the way. They were unexpectedly joined in sorrow. Nicodemus had available the spices for burial, but no tomb. Joseph had a place to bury Jesus and permission to take the body, but no preparations for embalming.

"Joseph of Arimathaea became the most privileged undertaker of all ages!" Henry G. Bosch has said. In the embalming process he and his assistant, Nicodemus, took Jesus' bruised body gently from the cross and wrapped it in a clean cloth. Then they wound the body in additional "linen clothes with the spices, as the manner of the Jews is to bury" (John 19:40) and placed him in Joseph's new tomb.

Reverently, they did what they could for a respectful burial of the body of our Lord.

Their actions raised many questions in their lives, as men of position have great responsibility. The higher one rises the more is demanded of him and the more he is watched. He is above the crowd for all to see. This became true of Joseph and Nicodemus.

These two men could have done much if they had come forward earlier. Gamaliel, another member of the Sanhedrin, later did some effective things for the gospel. But when they came at last, they made their confession public. They were "bearing his reproach" when they showed their loyalty to Christ, exposing themselves to ridicule and persecution.

They surely loved Jesus to make such a break with tradition and such a demand upon Pilate. They defied the prejudices of the chief priests. They gave Jesus a new tomb and prepared him for burial like a loved one rather than a crucified criminal.

We can't disregard the courage of these men at this moment. We have to respect it. The heart's glimpse of Christ on the cross can turn the fearful into heroes and the timid into aggressive witnesses.

It is always true that to have the blessing and joy of salvation there must be a confession. These two men waited until he was dead. They never heard "Well done!" from the living lips of Jesus when he needed their friendship, their approving and loving words.

Some like to talk about secret discipleship in our time. Let me remind you that the only thing the secret disciples were known for in the Bible is for burying Jesus. Is that how you wish to be remembered? Just for burying Jesus?

In contrast, a forgiven and sensitive woman broke her alabaster box and anointed Jesus for his burial several days before he died. Jesus said of her that "She hath done what she could; she is come beforehand to anoint my body to the burying, Verily I say unto you, Wherever this gospel shall be preached throughout the whole world, this also that she hath done shall be spoken of for a memorial of her" (Mark 14:8–9).

Nicodemus anointed Jesus after his death, but Jesus was not alive to praise him. Searching the pages of the New Testament and looking at all the resurrection appearances of Jesus, we do not find the names of Nicodemus and Joseph mentioned.

Since their actions of courage were late, we must wait to hear in their behalf from the Master at the last day.

15
THOMAS
. . . who still doubted Him

"I Want to Believe!"
John 20:24–29

Ten years ago an actress, after a lifetime battle with alcohol and drugs as well as several attempts at suicide, was taken to a hospital emergency room. For the first time she pleaded, "I want to live!" It seemed a paradox, for up to that moment she had seemed bent on self-destruction.

Going through a discouraged mood, an apostle of Jesus expressed a similar positive desire: "I want to believe!" This was "Thomas the Doubter," and he was not having an easy time with it. His appellation has been written across the minds of men ever since the resurrection of Christ.

He is identified in the Scriptures by another name, Didymus, meaning "the twin"—*didymus* being the Greek word for twin.

Immediately this raises a question as to why it was necessary for them to use this additional description, as we would use a nickname. Some have suggested that his name was Judas Thomas. There was Judas Iscariot mentioned and another referred to as "Judas, not Iscariot."

Much legend has grown up about this man. It is believed that perhaps his life ended in Persia as a martyr of the faith. In A.D. 1500 some missionaries found in that area a church called "The

Church of Saint Thomas." It had existed so long there was no record how it came to be organized. In the first century, Persia was the one nation that the Romans respected and feared. It took great courage and faith to have served there.

Thomas was always asking questions. This may have been bothersome to the other disciples. Perhaps he was brash and sometimes crude and a little unkindly in rushing in and raising a question when it was not always timely. A question out of time makes a question out of place, it is said.

Thomas was not all bad, and he was not all doubter. He was just very human. He is like us in more than just doubts. Did not the other disciples also have their doubts? We are not talking about wholesome questioning. We speak of the resurrection experience in which Thomas shared the difficulty of believing with the other disciples.

They had heard from the women who went to the tomb the story that Jesus had risen. This seemed unbelievable. They had known that Jesus had power over death, for they had seen him raise the dead—the ruler's daughter, the young man in Nain, and Lazarus. But all of these were still mortal and would die again. Jesus came forth from the grave in a heavenly body.

The women who went to the tomb in the early morning came back saying: "We have seen the Lord! He is risen!"

It was the consensus among the disciples, according to Luke 24, that the women's words seemed as idle talk. There was still doubt in their minds.

There was the time Jesus appeared after the resurrection by the Sea of Galilee. Peter jumped out of the boat and went to him. The Bible said the disciples "yet believed not for joy, and wondered" (Luke 24:41).

Matthew, Mark, Luke, and the book of Acts are silent concerning Thomas Didymus, other than mentioning his name along with the other apostles. But John's Gospel gives three experiences which show Thomas' dilemma of doubt. All three times he was asking questions. However, through these questions we reconstruct what we know concerning the character of this apostle.

Courage

Doubting Thomas, he was. We do not disclaim this. He was slow to act, and belief did not come easy for him. When conviction came, he grasped it. He wanted to know. He wanted proof, and that's not a bad trait.

But never put this man down as anything less than courageous. In the eleventh chapter of John we see the raw courage of Thomas.

Jesus was ministering across the river Jordan, away from Jerusalem. They had been there two or three days. The disciples probably felt relieved that Jesus was safe from the growing animosity of the Jews.

Then a word of sorrow and heartbreak came: Lazarus was sick unto death. The disciples were afraid they knew exactly what Jesus would do. Had they taken a vote, they would have agreed that they should stay where they were, as Jesus' life would be in danger in Judea.

When Thomas found that Jesus was going back, with utter disregard for his own life Thomas said, "Let us also go, that we may die with him!" (John 11:16).

These were pessimistic words. But Thomas had evaluated the situation and to him it seemed a deathtrap. He felt they would be killed immediately if they returned to Bethany. That mattered nothing—if Jesus went, Thomas was going. That was boldness few men have—with doubt or without doubt.

Consolation

Thomas' courage finally led to consolation and comfort.

From Bethany, after the raising of Lazarus, Jesus moved closer to Jerusalem and the cross. In the upper room, the Master began to speak the tenderest words that came from his lips. We find in the fourteenth chapter of John what Matthew Henry called "Jesus' Last Will and Testament." The impact of those words mean so much to us we hardly notice that Thomas interrupted several times.

Jesus was trying to tell his disciples that he was actually going to die. Thomas could believe they were all going to get killed, but he didn't want Jesus to die! The Lord was preparing them for what would happen to him and to them. He concluded by saying, "Whither I go ye know, and the way ye know."

As usual, Thomas questioned. "Lord, we know not whither thou goest; and how can we know the way?" (John 14:5).

He didn't mind going anywhere with Jesus. He didn't really mind dying with Jesus. But he had come to the place in his courageous devotion that he did not want to live without Jesus.

When you put your hand to the plow and sense the joy and wonder of God's presence, then if the skies turn dark and you can no longer hear the voice of God, you feel there is little reason for living. Life holds nothing but bitterness. You taste the dregs of pessimism and raise questions—until you return to him who is the answer to all questions. In a way, Thomas was asking our questions.

Jesus didn't seem to consider Thomas an interrupter. Our Lord, who knew all thimgs, listened to him patiently and understood that Thomas needed his doubts removed.

"I am the way," Jesus said, "the truth, and the life: no man cometh unto the Father, but by me" (John 14:6).

"Ye believe in God," he declared. "Believe also in me." They were to look forward to heaven. "In my Father's house are many mansions: if it were not so, I would have told you. I go to prepare

a place for you. And if I go and prepare a place for you, I will come again" (John 14:1–2). They were given consolation and comfort in the hope of the return of Christ.

Thomas' questions were the same kind of questions we ask on a dark night, in a closed room, when nobody but God is listening.

Confession

When doubt is cleared up, it leads to renewed confession.

The evening of Christ's resurrection the disciples gathered behind closed doors. The rumors had been strange and confusing. They certainly were not expecting Jesus.

Formerly, in their togetherness had been strength, so they came together in hope that somebody had seen and heard something of Jesus that would give them encouragement. Quite unexpectedly, the risen Jesus appeared in their midst.

"But Thomas . . . was not with them when Jesus came" (John 20:24).

This verse is a powerful plea for faithful gathering with other believers for worship, prayer, and preaching of the Word. Thomas was not with the other disciples when Jesus came. Therefore he was deprived of the blessing of the Lord's presence.

The news got back to Thomas that Jesus had appeared to the others. He had missed it! The Scripture never gives any reason, any more than God honors our excuses today.

Thomas began to feel pressure. He envied the fact that they had seen and felt something that he had not.

"Except I shall see . . . the print of the nails," he said, "and put my finger into the print of the nails, and thrust my hand into his side, I will not believe" (John 20:25).

A week later Jesus confronted him. Listen to Thomas' confession! As soon as Thomas saw Jesus, he was no longer anxious to put his finger into Jesus' side. He fell on his face and exclaimed,

"My Lord and my God!" He made the good confession! confession
. . . the leap of faith.

Jesus said, to him and to us, "Because thou hast seen me, thou
hast believed: blessed are they that have not seen and yet have
believed" (John 20:29).